Unleashing the Truth

How To Be Intimate With God

Unleashing the Truth

How To Be Intimate With God

Clive E. Neil

END TIME WAVE
PUBLICATIONS

Bogota, New Jersey

Unleashing the Truth
How To Be Intimate With God

Typesetter: Sheila Chang
Proofreader: Sharon D. Motley

CONTENTS

FOREWORD

Harry Emerson Fosdick, hailed by some as the greatest preacher of the twentieth century, once offered a rather intriguing definition of preaching. "Preaching," mused Fosdick, "is counseling on a group scale." Such a definition, to be sure, betrays a certain bias, which is neither normative nor comprehensive. As a matter of fact, I find Fosdick's working definition of preaching both highly questionable and very objectionable. Pastoral Preaching and Pastoral Counseling are, after all, two distinct, though interrelated, enterprises, which articulate differing aims and employ different modalities. Thus, these two arts/sciences should never be confused with nor substituted for one another.

Nonetheless, I have made the Fosdickian citation not because I deem it definitive nor exhaustive. I have cited Fosdick because I believe his words offer, not a working definition of preaching in general, but rather a worthy description of the preaching of Dr. Clive E. Neil in particular. His preaching in effect, if not in intent, is "counseling on a group scale." As a matter of fact, anyone who has ever heard Dr. Neil will readily admit that his preaching is both therapeutic and transformative, cathartic and celebrative, without being compensatory. Indeed, Dr. Neil exhibits a unique, invaluable gift for and skill at interpreting human texts, divining the inner workings of the minds and the inchoate cravings of the hearts of his listeners. In short, he has an uncanny knack for scratching the existential, yet unique, itch of those who are fortunate enough to hear him.

Herein, however, permit me to hasten to clarify any misimpression which I have left about what I have said. I am in no way suggesting that whenever Dr. Neil mounts the pulpit of the Bedford Central Presbyterian Church that he does so as a therapist. On the contrary, whenever and wherever Dr. Neil preaches, be it at Bedford or elsewhere, he brings with him not the pen and pad of a therapist, but rather the "shoes of a preacher," to put it in the vernacular of the Black Church. He stands and speaks as a preacher, an able interpreter of the sacred text, who evidences that he has both heard and heeded the pastoral admonition, "Study to shew thyself approved unto God, a workman that needeth not be ashamed, rightly dividing the truth" (II Tim. 2:15).

In this volume of sermons, <u>Unleashing the Truth</u>, Dr. Neil continues to investigate and illuminate themes which were first given voice to in his initial work, <u>Developing Healthy Relationships</u>. In this volume, Neil offers the grace and guidance of the Gospel of Jesus Christ to those who hope for and grope towards an answer to the preeminent questions on the minds and profoundest stirrings in the hearts of saints and sinners alike: Where can I find authentic experiences of genuine intimacy and communion? The answer which Dr. Neil gives to this question hinges on his core conviction that penultimate matters, individual addressed in the light of Ultimate Reality, the Christian God. In other words, one cannot operate at the optimal level of functioning nor fulfillment until he/she has entered into a deep, dynamic relationship with the Almighty. What I appreciate most about this volume, however, is that Dr. Neil does not simply tell his listeners/readers what to do, contrary, he shows them how to do so.

What Henri Nouwen says of most Christian leaders in general, I maintain, is true of many preachers in particular: "Much Christian Leadership is exercised by people who do not know how to develop a healthy intimate relationship." I firmly believe that what makes Dr. Clive Neil so insightful to and helpful for others is that Dr. Neil shares what he has searched for and secured: real intimacy with others through real intimacy with God who continues to incarnate and reveal Godself within the context of human relationships. In other words, Dr. Neil speaks with authority and authenticity because he not only has spent sufficient time training "to talk and be with people" as a pastoral counselor, but also because he logs daily/weekly sufficient time training his head and heart to talk and to be with God.

This volume of sermons, while preached principally at and to the members of Bedford Central, is one from which both the churched and unchurched, the pulpit and the pew, can benefit. This volume of sermons will be of interest and help to anyone who hungers for a functional, fulfilling relationship; for anyone who wishes to continue to grow in the grace and wisdom of the Lord Jesus Christ.

Rev. Anthony L. Trufant, Senior Pastor
Emmanuel Baptist Church
Brooklyn, New York
April 23, 1996

INTRODUCTION

Can you imagine building a house without an architect's carefully drawn plans? The kitchen might end up in the dining room, the living room would probably have the washer and dryer connections sticking out of the fireplace, and who knows what effect that would have on the wiring. Flip the light switch on in the master bedroom, and the oven would start to preheat. This is probably not the kind of place in which you would want to spend the rest of your life.

No reasonable person would think of building a house without the meticulous plans of an architect. And yet, people regularly attempt to build their relationships without consulting the Master Architect of that relationship. We rely instead on sketchy blueprints we receive from our parents and the world around us. The result is two people under the same roof hammering away to build a model marriage based on two different sets of plans. This may sound confusing but it is true. This is why so many couples end up with such poorly constructed marriages. Take a look and you will see that their love has faded, their commitment is crumbling, and the communication is wired all wrong— the foundation is cracked and the roof is sagging, getting ready to cave in. Who wants to spend the rest of their life in a disaster area? No one. That is why so many people don't. They choose instead to declare their marriage condemned and demolish it.

Are there any alternatives? Yes, we can put away our amateur ideas of how to build a good marriage and start remodeling based on the blueprint found in God's Word. I must warn you though that it won't be easy. Rebuilding is not that simple. In fact, anyone who has tried to refurbish a home recognizes the following:

1. It takes longer than you planned.

2. It costs more than you estimated.

3.   It is messier than first anticipated and,

4.   It requires greater determination than expected.

What is true of our human relationship is also true of our relationship with God. It too will probably take longer, cost more, at times be messy, and require greater determination than expected. But the rewards and the blessings outweigh the cost tenfold.

The issue between staying together and dissolving a relationship is based on choice. There will be one recurring theme throughout this book and that is the issue of choice. We will be discussing the various ways we can enhance our relationship with God by the choices we make.

It is imperative that we remember that a love relationship is only as good as the needs it fulfills in each partner. It is also essential that there be a commonly understood language between each partner. For instance, between us and God one word that must be comprehended is love. Although it has been said that "fools explain it, but wise people never try," my experience has been the opposite.

There is a difference between being in love and actually loving someone. If love is reciprocated, the difference between these two conditions doesn't really matter. In other words, it is far easier to go from being in love to loving when your love is returned, for you and the person you love derive comfort from loving each other. Love in its truest form has both passion and comfort.

Being in love often involves passion without comfort and can have little to do with the actual object of your affection, other than your obsession with that person. Perhaps your love is not reciprocated and/or you demand that the other person love you in return. Unrequited love, the stuff which songs, plays, books, and movies are made of, can often lead to rage, suspicion, jealousy, and many varieties of distress. This kind of one-sided relationship is very common. The reality is that nobody can make another person love him or her. Throughout history, that truth has been a source of pain for countless numbers of people. If you have suffered this kind of pain, there is good news: to learn to focus your love on an appropriate partner, you must first be willing to deal with the issues that prevent you from loving. In my experience, practically everyone has the capacity to feel love for another person. But the ability to feel comfort as well as passion with another person involves more than just feeling love. It means loving— and there are many dimensions to that word.

There are two aspects I would like to attempt to define as each relates to the remainder of this book.

The first one that is woven into the fabric of this book is commitment. Commitment has become a buzzword that describes the process by which each person defines his or her desire for a long-term relationship rather than a short-term relationship. But the concept and the word itself are covered with discrepancies and ambiguities.

We hear a great deal these days about people who cannot commit to a relationship. But I have come to see that many who have been perceived as unable to commit in one relationship appear to "spontaneously recover" when starting the next. Once the unsuccessful relationship ended, the next relationship with a new partner seemed to trigger few of the issues that had been present in the previous one.

It is said that intimacy is the crying need of the human heart. But when you ask people to define intimacy, they hem and haw trying to come up with words that work. Our working definition in this book for commitment is the cooperative agreement that exists between the two partners to stay together under the rules that they have established for themselves until one or both persons change their minds. Christians are called upon to be both intimate and committed to God.

The second aspect is intimacy. Intimacy is the ability to share your innermost self with another person. Sometimes, but not always, this means opening that part of yourself which no one else has access to. No universal definition exists which determines the right amount of intimacy. All relationships ultimately develop their own depth and style of intimacy. The degree to which you are able to establish this crucial intimacy in your relationship can usually be measured by your comfort level as a couple. Indeed, the real intimacy which many couples experience takes place not in the bedroom but in the living room.

In this book we will consider intimacy in its broadest sense. I agree that intimacy means sharing many secrets— but it also means sharing many of the common, everyday humdrum matters of life. The ability to communicate about the widest range of subjects and concerns is what enhances your growth in a relationship.

The concept of intimacy has been so used, abused, and misused today that you can put almost anything under it, and it will work. That is because most people are desperately looking for love in all the wrong places. They know they need it, they know they've got to have it, but where to find it and how to know it's authentic is another issue.

If you can relate to these feelings or know someone else who does, I have good news for you. God would like to develop an intimate relationship with you. I know you have heard this many times before, but I hope that by the end of this book the little phrase "I love you" will take on a new world of meaning to you.

The love of God is the joyful, self-determination to reflect the goodness of God's will and glory by meeting the needs of humanity. That is a big definition, but I believe it includes the key elements of what the Bible means by God's love. The Bible makes this absolutely clear: no definition of intimacy means anything unless it is rooted in God. No matter how we define intimacy, if we cannot root our definition in God, it is flawed. It will either be incomplete or unbalanced, but it will not be correct because God is the definition of intimacy. Our attempt to be intimate will not find the harmony and wholeness it can enjoy until we anchor it in God.

God's desire to be intimate reflects His determination to ensure the comprehensive welfare of His children. God loves us in such a way that God is not just concerned about getting us to heaven. He also cares about our comprehensive well-being, every minute detail of our lives. Being intimate with God means we have God's guarantee that in every situation in life, He loves us. When our world falls apart, we can say to God "I don't know why I'm going through this. I don't understand it, but I'm sure you love me." When we have someone holding us, who is intimate with us, it doesn't matter anymore what everyone else does. When we are in the arms of a loving God and become consumed with His love, God holds us and says "Don't cry. I am here. I love you."

The following excerpts were written with God's desire to be intimate with us in mind. There are too many of us who have solid interests and find great joy in our worldly pleasures; however, when it comes to our relationship with God there is a nonchalantness about how close we get to Him. This is often contingent upon our life circumstances. It is time to get on the same wavelength with God and learn to love Him in the way which God desires to be loved. Come and explore these sermons which outline the various ways we can develop an intimate relationship with God and start enjoying a love partnership which is unbelievable.

ACKNOWLEDGEMENTS

Most of these sermons were preached from the pulpit of the Bedford-Central Presbyterian Church. I would like to thank the members of this great church for their openness to God's Word and their willingness to demonstrate His Word in practical ways. To my wife Faye, daughter Aisha and son Darius, I owe a tremendous amount of gratitude for allowing me space to think and write. To Cecilia Channell-Cherry and Charmaine Massiah for their excellent editorial assistance in the preparation of this manuscript. To my parents for their constant support and prayers: thanks for the foundation that you laid for me to build on.

CHAPTER I

HOW TO LOVE GOD

Now these are the commandments, the statutes, and the judgments, which the LORD your God commanded to teach you, that ye might do them in the land whither ye go to possess it:

That thou mightest fear the LORD thy God, to keep all his statutes and his commandments, which I command thee, thou, and thy son, and thy son's son, all the days of thy life; and that thy days may be prolonged.

Hear therefore, O Israel, and observe to do it; that it may be well with thee, and that ye may increase mightily, as the LORD God of thy fathers hath promised thee, in the land that floweth with milk and honey.

Hear, O Israel: The LORD our God is one LORD:

And thou shalt love the LORD thy God with all thine heart, and with all thy soul, and with all thy might.
Deuteronomy 6:1-5

My Pastor in Philadelphia said that one day he asked the Lord, "Why do we have to go to church all the time? What's the problem? Why can't we preach once and have the message stick?" He said the Lord reminded him of the character of people. We are like sheep so easily diverted, who go astray from our original intent. No one who is a serious Christian plans on leaving God out; it just happens in the hustle and bustle of the day or moment. We get busy and God slips out of our thoughts until we are reminded somewhere down the line about our God.

One of the problems about an intimate relationship with God is knowing how to love God. We have a problem with the concept of love in general, because most of us don't know how to love. When we look at relationships in the home, it reminds us if you can't love the people you see every day, then you can't talk God's love yet. For it is in the ability to love God that provides the input for living. If we have not yet learned to love God then we have missed out on love.

The Bible declares that God is love, and it assumes then some understanding of God, if we are to understand love. If we do not understand a love relationship with God, then we do not understand love. Moreover, if we do not understand love, how can we love that which we do not understand? So, if we are not alive today, it is because we have not learned to love God. People are trying to love life without loving God, yet wondering how they are always missing out. Moses speaks to Israel through the Word of God about loving God. When we love God we learn to love. Moses is writing to the children of Israel as they prepare to go into the promised land. **He said this is the commandment, the statutes, which the Lord has commanded me to teach you. He told me to tell you God knows that His people have a problem, and that when God gives a land of milk and honey, we tend to forget where it comes from. Though we may thank God at first, it keeps coming, so we assume it is supposed to keep coming.**

The reason why God wants to pull us back to His love is to remind us that what we have and who we are is a continuous flow from Him.

In Deuteronomy 6, verses 4-5 make up what is called the "Jewish Schema" because it is the recitation of what was said twice a day. "Hear O Israel— the Lord your God is one! You shall love the Lord God with all your heart, with all your soul, and with all your might. Bind them, and teach them." God knows how forgetful we are, so He starts out with why we should love God, in

His power. If I should read the Hebrew it would say "Hear O Israel, Jehovah is your Elohim." There are two names for God. One is Elohim, which speaks of God in His power as awesome. The reason Israel had a land to go to is that God in His power is awesome. The Walls of Jericho fell down— because God is awesome. The reason we are here today is— God is awesome. Psalm 139 shows that God's handiwork has put us together like this world had never seen— Elohim. A second name— Jehovah— speaks of God in relationship to humanity. God is not only transcendent, and awesome, but also God is the one who wants to have a relationship with us. God, who created the world, said I want you to have My love and I want us to be lovers, to fall in love with Him.

We find that God Almighty, who doesn't need anyone or anything, approaches everyone and asks, "do you mind if we develop a love relationship?" It was so awesome that God wanted to be so close to Israel that He told them to remember it all day long. This was unusual since God is independent. He sits outside of time and space, without need for time and space, and is in control of time and space. God is not in need of us. He doesn't have to do anything but He wants to do it. With this in mind, how can you turn down someone like God? He tells you to start your day off right, for the God who created you wants to have a relationship with you.

We ought to love God. Why? Because He is God, the Powerful Creator. He wants a relationship with each of us so that we may be close to Him, and He to us. Therefore, He said that we are to love Him with all of our heart, soul and might. However, our immediate problem with this commandment is our lack of understanding of what it means to love. We find in our culture, love is like a Milky Way candy bar or a milkshake. It is a snappy, emotional love without depth. The Bible says God is love, so in order to define love we need to get God's definition. We cannot get this definition from "As the World Turns," neither can we get it from "All My Children," nor "Martin Lawrence." We need God's definition of love, for He is our only help.

When God defines love He defines it as one's commitment to do the highest good for the one he or she loves. Love involves commitment. When a person says "I love you, but I'm not ready to marry you," he/she is actually saying "I am not ready to make a commitment because love is equivalent to commitment." People want to experience the fun of love without the responsibility of love. Therefore, they do not learn the meaning of love. Love starts with a commitment to do for the other person anything and everything. It is not a commitment to self first, but on the contrary, it is a commitment to the other person first. So often, we focus on that which we will get for ourselves, how will we benefit. Love asks the question "What am I going to do for him/her so that I can become all that God wants me to be?" With this definition, what does it mean to love God? If loving means to seek the highest good of the one loved— how does one seek the highest good of God? Glorify Him. The highest good that we can express to God is to seek His glory in all of life. To make a conscious, intelligent decision to love God is a willingness to personally reflect every day the character of God. Loving God is a commitment of life. Love is more than a feeling; therefore, a person may say "I don't feel like I love him/her anymore" and what this means is that the feeling has changed thus the love is gone. In this situation, I wonder what the person is committed to do in order to get the feeling back. Love is the commitment to act whether the feeling comes or goes. It is our nature to act on the feeling. However, what if God had waited for "the feeling?" He would never have sent His Son. What if Jesus waited for "the feeling;" He never would have died on the cross. Hence there would be no salvation.

How does God want us to love Him? There are three ways: with all of our heart, all of our soul, and all of our might. Notice that it says "all." In the New Testament He said with all your mind.

1.	The first thing is *Love Me with all of your heart*. In the Bible, the heart means the CORE of something. It is the center channel whereby something can be identified, the inner nature of a thing. When a person says that he or she loves you with their heart, what is implied is that the love for you is more than anything else in their possession. This means that there is one beyond what you see, the one that lives inside, and from the core you are loved. When you tell someone that you love them, it is not that you love him or her in the things that you do but it's that you love in the essence of who you are. This is what God is asking, for He just doesn't want your physical bodies or your ears open. Rather, He wants to know if the very essence of you belongs to Him. How would you answer this: Do you love God from the center of your being? Keep in mind that distance sets in if He does not have the core of your life.

2.	*Love Me with all of your soul*. This is difficult since soul is used for a number of things in the Bible. One of its first usages is in Creation— "And God breathed in Man the breath of life and he became a living soul." It was not until God breathed in him that he started living. Soul means a special kind of self awareness. Do you remember when you were first in love, how you would think about yourself and immediately think about him/her? It was automatic to think of the other person. Now, it doesn't matter if that first love comes or goes. What happened is that you have separated self-awareness from selfish love. Selfish love says that I want to relate to me as I relate to you. What God is asking is that He be a part of/take part in everything you have to do— to the point where there are no decisions, plans, orientation that would not involve God. One way in which you know you are growing in the love of God is when you automatically include God to be in on all you do.

3.	*Love Me with all of your might.* Love is a full time job. It is a lot of work. When you choose to love, you make a decision to work. Folks say "back when we were ...it wasn't hard before..." because there was no responsibility. Love is hard work.

You have to decide that you are going to work for the rest of your life. Hard work is trying to know someone else. Hard work is spending your time with someone else. Hard work is understanding someone else. It is hard work knowing someone else's likes and dislikes. The only way to survive is to study the object of our love. This is the nature of God's love— when it comes to loving God we have to decide to go to work. Usually, we tend to give God time when there is no more television to watch, or just before bed. We don't give God the hard work that is necessary. We must say "God, here is Your time"— and make time to study and to pray. Love is when you don't feel like you have to do it because it is work. For example, a husband and wife may argue because one is hearing but not listening; therefore, one says "when you come back from where you are, then we can talk." This is exactly what happens between us and God. At this point, God asks "which of you have heard My words but you are not listening?" Are you listening to the point where it compels you to act?

What makes us want to work? Usually, it is because of the values we have placed on having something. If we receive a call in the dead of night to come downtown to collect $30,000, how quickly we would get dressed and go— because there is something of value there that you want obviously more than your sleep. God says, "until we decide that we greatly value our time with Him, we will never receive the corresponding energy to know Him." Loving God is an effort and decision of the will and not a feeling of emotion. Some of us are still waiting to love God— but it will never happen in such a way. I challenge you, right now, to make an appointment with God and keep it.

CHAPTER II

HONORING GOD

Trust in the LORD with all thine heart; and lean not unto thine own understanding.

In all thy ways acknowledge him, and he shall direct thy paths.

Be not wise in thine own eyes: fear the LORD, and depart from evil.

It shall be health to thy navel, and marrow to thy bones.

Honour the LORD with thy substance, and with the firstfruits of all thine increase:

So shall thy barns be filled with plenty, and thy presses shall burst out with new wine.

Proverbs 3:5-10

Proverbs are statements of wisdom providing instructions on living a godly life. The proverbs are common sense phrases that should be characteristic of a wise person. Verse 9 begins by telling us to honor God with our wealth and the first of all our produce. God's Church today has every right to address these verses. If there is one fellowship that does not display a love for money, it should be the fellowship among God's children. Our love is to be for people, but when the Bible speaks about the visible proof of one's private commitment— we are challenged to be just as loving with our personal possessions. A repetitive theme throughout the Scriptures is how one handles personal wealth. How a person handles their money is often displayed as the sincerity of their commitment to God. The reason this issue comes up is because God knows, as we know, that the dollar is the last thing we want to give up. A person will sooner give up his spouse than his dollar. People kill for money. A dice game on the corner that is worth a dollar can produce bloodshed, because of the value man places on money itself. The value one places on God is not only reflected in their praise to God with their lips, or their presence before God in His worship, but also reflected in their honoring God in their giving. Therefore, these two verses (9 and 10) come to us from Solomon in a very uncomfortable way, addressing a very uncomfortable subject.

When we observe nature, we will find that everything God creates honors Him by giving. God created the sun, and we live by the sunlight which He has enabled it to give daily. God created the moon, it gives brightness at night. God created the stars, they give radiance to the sky. He created the earth and it gives nutrients to the crops. God created the animal kingdom and they give, for much of what we wear is based on what His creation has given. How the sea gives back to Him is reflected on our plates at dinner time. It is people, however, whose selfishness detains them from giving or they misuse giving. People cannot see that God not only gave that we might enjoy, but He gave that we might also learn to give. So He says, "Honor the Lord with your wealth and with the firstfruit of your produce— so your barn will be filled with plenty and vats that overflow." It is not surprising that we like verse 10, and if given a choice, we memorize verse 10 and bypass verse 9.

To honor means to hold something in highest esteem; lifting it up so that it is recognized to be very valuable, giving something ultimate significance. Children, honor your parents. Honor your mother and father; hold them up with high regard. You don't need to agree with them, but there should never be a time when mom and dad are not lifted up with high esteem. Young people are to honor their elders. They may not do things your way and you may consider them old fashioned, but they are still your elders and deserve to be given recognition as such. Unfortunately, we have lost this element in our culture today. That is one reason why titles were used for older persons, such as Mr. Smith, not Samuel, to give the esteem and high regard that goes with a name. Children of God, Peter and Paul admonished us to honor those who teach us giving them esteem. They are not saying that they are better than you, but there should be recognition for the position in life that God has given them. My daddy reminds me that I have to respect his wishes as long as I am under his roof. Under his roof he calls the shots, and I must submit to that. He demands to be respected under his roof. The Bible validates the Scripture which says "Honor the Lord, hold Him with high esteem." He is more than a big brother in the sky, or big daddy upstairs. He is the Lord, the Creator of heaven and earth, and the Bible says we are to honor Him. He is the Creator, sustainer of the universe, and His creation ought to honor Him.

How does one honor the Lord? There are a number of ways: praise, worship, presence, service, and witness. But here, Solomon gives a specific way. He says to honor the Lord from your wealth. The esteem you feel for God is reflected in what you give back to Him. A person demonstrates how much value they put on God by what they give. God looks at what He has given us and then looks at what we have given back. Based on this, God measures our honor of Him in how we express our thanksgiving to Him. The value that I express to my parents is in appreciation of their raising me, and I express this by giving them my time, energy and support. When Solomon says to honor the Lord with your wealth, he says to recognize that wealth is a reflection of God's gift to you, and your appreciation of Him who gave it is reflected in what you do in return. So your act of giving freely and unselfishly is the specific aspect of what Solomon means to honor the Lord.

The reality is that we live in a time when God is no longer honored in this way. We live in a time of gimmicks and gadgetry, in a time where people have to be manipulated and tricked into honoring God. Songs and dance shows have to be performed in order for us to tell God that He is special— and this should not be. Solomon says God is something special because He is God. You honor the Lord because He is the Lord. Many of our parents didn't have to do anything for us. They raised us— and they should be honored. The fact that God is God should produce in His people a desire to honor Him. The way we do that, says Solomon, is when we give back to God out of our wealth.

At this point, the common question arises about Solomon's instruction to honor God from the "first" of our produce. The doctrine of firstfruits says that when anything grows in your garden, the first portion belongs to God. You are not to give your family and friends first and then give God the leftovers. Firstfruits says that before you even enjoy any of it, you are to give God His portion. This doctrine demands that you recognize the fact that everything comes from God's ground, and because of God's weather, God provided the nutrients that cause the produce to grow. Therefore, it is appropriate that you give God first. Giving God firstfruit means giving God the best of the produce. Notice in verse 10, he is not saying give to God and God will give to you. He said honor God and God will give to you in the manner in which you honor God. In giving God firstfruits, you are doing so in the spirit that says "I start with God and end with God."

I suspect if I were God I would do the same thing, just to remind people where their sustenance comes from. This reminds me of the little boy given 50 cents for Sunday school. His mother said, "Son, one quarter is for you and the other quarter is for God." He had the quarters in his hand and while running, he tripped. One of the quarters rolled down the street into a pond and the other fell on the ground. The little boy went over, picked up the quarter and said, "Well, God there goes your quarter." This is the attitude that is fostered in our day when we are accustomed to giving God our leftovers. That is why Paul said on the first day of the week lay aside to yourself. It is unacceptable to God for a person to sit in worship, open their wallet or purse and have nothing to give. The Bible says you did not think about Me. Paul says you are to lay it aside before you come to worship because you think about how you got it.

This same concept is found in the Lord's prayer. You begin by saying "Our Father which art in Heaven," then you say, "give us this day our daily bread." Honoring God starts with a focus on Him. We only have what we have because God gave it to us. He gave to us so we might honor Him. Honoring God is placing God in the place of high esteem. Someone once said there needs to be a development of a cure for "sclerosis of the giver." This disease was discovered by a husband and wife team of doctors. It is a condition that renders the patient's hand immobile when he/she is tempted to reach in the direction of the wallet or purse. Miraculously, this condition is absent in supermarkets, on the golf course, and even in shopping malls and restaurants. The best cure for this condition is to get the individual's heart right with God. A good dosage of Romans 12:1 or Luke 9:35 will be quite pleasing if swallowed with Malachi 3:10 or Philippians 3:19.

People have lost focus of why we should honor God. God says to honor Him because He is, and you have what you have strictly because the Lord has provided. In the Old Testament, the believers who wanted to honor God looked at how much more they could give. When we honor God in our giving, we seek new ways and greater ways to do more. The Bible says that if we only understood the grace of God, no one would talk about giving— but the attitude would be "how much more Lord?" How can we say thanks? We must first understand how far God's grace has brought us, then we would be grateful. We have been made so free by grace that we take it for granted.

Many people wish they had lived in the Old Testament times when God spoke audibly to people. The Bible says all they had was a shadow of things to come. Every time they blew it, they had to offer a sacrifice. Day by day they lived knowing that what they did today could not help them tomorrow. Each day they lived under the burden of the law. They could not keep it and neither can we, but it is being kept for us. God is satisfied with the keeper of the law— Jesus Christ. When we are satisfied with Christ, we don't need to make sacrifices. We just need to call on the name of

Christ and God is satisfied. We have so much more under grace and yet we have shifted our priorities. Everything has become more important than our gift to God. God should be our greatest claim to fame.

My greatest claim to fame is that I am living forever.

My greatest claim is that I know Christ.

My greatest claim is God says He loves me and I love Him.

The Bible says to honor the Lord. The tragedy is the more we earn, the more we believe we did it by our own hand. Solomon says when you start, start with the God who provides. A man came to his pastor one day, convicted that he was not giving to God a portion of his thousand dollars per week salary. The man said, "I had no problem giving to God when I was making fifty dollars per week. Please pray for me. I make one hundred times that, and it's a problem now for me to give to God." The pastor bowed his head and prayed, "Lord, bring this man back to making fifty dollars a week so he can start giving back like he used to."

We have sinned against God— in our attempts to honor Him. God wants to be honored, and to honor God is to express to Him that we recognize that everything comes from Him. Some of us should be ashamed of our giving. We give him $1 when we should be giving $10. Then you look at your household, and you see what God has provided. How can you consider the education He allowed you to get and the opportunities He made available to you, and then sit in His presence and insult Him. The widow who gave all she had honored Jesus by giving something valuable. God says, "If you want filled barns and overflowing vats, give to Me." God deserves the best since God gave us His best— His Son.

CHAPTER III

A PERSPECTIVE ON LOVE

For the love of Christ constraineth us; because we thus judge, that if one died for all, then were all dead:

And that he died for all, that they which live should not henceforth live unto themselves, but unto him which died for them, and rose again.

Wherefore henceforth know we no man after the flesh: yea, though we have known Christ after the flesh, yet now henceforth know we him no more.

Therefore if any man be in Christ, he is a new creature: old things are passed away; behold, all things are become new.

And all things are of God, who hath reconciled us to himself by Jesus Christ, and hath given to us the ministry of reconciliation;

To wit, that God was in Christ, reconciling the world unto himself, not imputing their trespasses unto them; and hath committed unto us the word of reconciliation.

II Corinthians 5:14-19

What is the perspective of true commitment? What goes through our minds when we say that we are in love with God? Anybody who attends church talks God-talk. But when God analyzes our love for Him, He wants to know not only what's on our lips but also what's in our heads and hearts.

True love determines the goals and the motivation for our lives. I am not saying that true love comes easily. There are few things that we possess or that we enjoy which didn't cost us something to obtain them. Surely, there are things that you have which cost something— whether it be a college degree which you had to go to school and earn or a career that you had to work for. Yet, isn't it funny that when it comes to our commitment to the Lord— the one whom we say we love the most— the price is too high to pay? Evidently, we have a perspective problem.

There was a great Jewish leader, a representative of the Sanhedrin to the people of his day, who had a perspective problem. Paul, a powerful man in Judaism during his time, was confronted by the Christ on the Damascus road. Whenever you read his writings, he constantly reflects back to what happened there. On that day when he was blinded on the Damascus road, he actually started to see. That day, Paul said God grabbed him for a higher purpose. Whenever you hear from Paul, he proclaims the same message: "I pressed on to the high calling of the mark in Christ Jesus. I run the race with patience. I beat my body under subjection." Paul became obsessed with a love for God. So he says "to the Jews, I became a Jew; to the Gentiles, I became a Gentile so I might win some." Paul had perspective.

As he received death threats from the people, Paul boasted, "For me to die is gain." He was told he couldn't live; Paul said that's okay, for me to live is Christ. In the face of suffering, Paul professed that the suffering of this present life cannot be compared with the joy that is to come. The people couldn't kill Paul and they couldn't hurt him because in every situation Christ came forth. Why? Paul had perspective.

What was that perspective? It was one that caused Paul to tell us in II Corinthians 5:18 that if we are beside ourselves it is for God. The people were saying that he was mad. Paul, who was so well connected in Judaism, gave it all up to serve Christ. "The man is beside himself. He is crazy, gone off the deep end, stupid, ignorant!" Every now and then someone ought to tell us that we are crazy; that we have gone out of our minds. If nobody ever notices your unique excitement for Christ, then something is wrong. For Paul, the commitment to Christ meant he was going against the norms of his culture. Paul writes that he was shipwrecked, abused, and constantly threatened for the sake of Christ.

Why is it okay for the world to get beside themselves over sports or television programs, but we can't get excited about Jesus? Paul says if we are beside ourselves (behave against the world's norms), it is for God— and that is a good reason. So he says get mad, but do it with sound judgment. So if in your church the choir sings and they are beside themselves— we should understand what they are mad about. And if the preacher gets so excited that you don't know what he's talking about— it's madness in a positive sense. Paul says I'm mad about God but you can not make sense of it.

Why is Paul mad, crazy for Christ, gone overboard suffering loss to follow Christ? Verse 14 of 2 Corinthians. Chapter 5 gives the motivational perspective of true love. It states that the love of Christ controls me, for One died for all so all died. The motivating thing that kept Paul was the love of Christ. One of the problems in Christianity that is evident in churches is that we have yet to learn about the love of Christ. Many of us function out of improper motives that have nothing to do with the love of Christ.

GUILT

One motive could be guilt. We feel guilty if we don't go to church on Sunday morning. We live Christian lives negatively because of how guilty we feel. If the primary motivation for why we serve the Christ is guilt, then we missed the opportunity to enjoy the full expression of our faith.

TRADITION

A second motive could be tradition. Being raised in the Church has instilled a habit in us to go every Sunday. It is a good tradition, but it is not sufficient to cause us to be a mad person for Christ. This is exactly why such a person can go away to college and leave the church, forgetting all that was "taught" while they were there. Suddenly college life seems better than the life back home with its traditions. Tradition doesn't hold you long if something more exciting comes along.

FEAR

A third improper motive is fear. Many people come to Christ because they are afraid of hell, and that's a good reason— but it is not good enough. If Christianity is nothing else for us but fire insurance, then we miss the focus. The thought behind such fear is that if you don't go to church or read the Bible then something will happen to you.

CULTURE

Culture is a fourth reason for why we serve Christ. It is the sophisticated thing to do, since every "good" American goes to church.

REWARD

Finally, reward is a big reason— let's make a deal with God and give Him something because we expect something in return.

All of these reasons have their place in understanding our motives, but then Paul gives us the true motivation. Paul says it ought to be the love of Christ, which should be so potent that it controls us. This love ought to be the steering wheel that maneuvers our lives. Unless it is the love of Christ which controls us, we will never be motivated properly to live for Christ and be what Christ created us to be.

The question then is what does that mean? "Love" in our culture is based on what we can get. Biblical love is based on the premise that I do what's best for another even if it costs me. "For God so loved the world that He gave His only begotten Son, that whoever believes in Him shall not perish but have everlasting life."

Paul says I am controlled by the love of Christ. What does he mean? My love for Christ or Christ's love for me? The answer is both. It is His love for me that produces my love for Him. And when His love for me combines with my love for Him, there is dynamite love. I am possessed for Christ. I understand His love for me and I respond back to Him in love. The two loves converge and explode and thus I am controlled! I am possessed for Christ.

What makes that love explosive? What's missing so we don't think he is possessed that way? We have misplaced or forgotten what Christ has done for us. Look at what Paul says: I am controlled having concluded this, that One died for all, therefore all died. He makes that statement so simply, yet we miss the point. For Paul, the death of Christ was not a foreign event 2000 years ago. It was real to him. The reason we lose the impact of the death of Christ is that we forget what took place on Calvary. Calvary became a tradition. We need to understand what Paul meant when he said "I have to keep what happened on the Cross in front of me, and when I do, my love converges with that love and produces a controlling love." For Paul, the fact that the God of the universe would come down to die was astronomical, especially since he knew that God did it for him!

When we consider the importance of Christ's grace and mercy for us, we need to realize that God didn't have to do it, didn't need to do it, but wanted to do it because He loves us. Unless we understand this, the love of Christ will wane. It is for this reason that we should spend a part of each day thanking God.

For most of us, our prayers consist of give me, give me, give me, and I want, I want, I want... Lord, you know I need, I need, I need. We have to thank God for what took place on Calvary. Paul realized that God loved him and died for him.

What motivates you? Is it the love of Christ or is it the feeling that you're under the pressure of being watched, or do you feel guilty? or is it because you have fallen in love with the Christ? To love Christ means that we are so thankful that we are motivated to want to please Him. This leads to a goal! The reason so many of us who love Christ never get going is we never have a goal. If we shoot for nothing, we will more than likely hit it every time. Paul understood that there was a goal to life. Christ died that they who lived should no longer live for themselves but for Him who died and rose on their behalf.

What does Paul say is the reason for living? For most people the reason for living is self-centeredness. Paul says that if the reason is based on self, we have missed the point. Most of the frustration and emptiness of life is due to the fact that people have decided to live for themselves. They soon find out that such living is miserable. Paul says the reason I am turned on in the morning is that I understand from the moment I open my eyes, I have a reason for living. Personally, my reason for living goes beyond my having to go to work, taking care of my family, loving my wife, and being a preacher. My reason for living is "to turn Christ on." So, now when I go to work my performance is affected because everything I do is done in the spirit and strength of Christ to glorify my God.

What we have done is to make the blessings of God an end in themselves. Therefore, we go to work to accumulate; we love our spouses to have nice families; we do things to get personal benefit. Paul says the goal of life— the reason we are alive— is "to turn God on," to please Him. In I Cor. 10:31, Paul says it this way: whether you eat or drink or whatever you do, do all to the glory of God. This may sound routine but Paul says we dare not sit down to a meal and think the reason we are eating is just to satisfy our appetite. There is a deeper purpose. When we say grace, we are letting God know that we've turned Him on. We are praising Him for all He gives to us.

When you do something for God, there are benefits. When you thank God for a meal, your stomach gets satisfied. When you perform a day's work, the employer is satisfied. There are benefits but you don't do them for the benefit— do them for God and He will *give* the benefits. We go off track when we think He should bless us because we have done things in the Church. When we do this we have just proven that we are not serving God out of the right motivation.

The right motivation is thankfulness for what He did on Calvary. If God never does anything else for me, He has already given me enough reason to serve Him. And God, in response to this kind of spirit says, "because you love Me enough to be so thankful I will freely give you all things." God is not a business person. He's not here to cut a deal with us. He wants a love relationship with each of us.

I can relate to verse 16. When I used to see people and noticed the car they were driving; the clothes they were wearing; the house they lived in— I looked at life secularly. But now I am in love with Christ, and I no longer see the one's external content because I have learned to look beneath, for spiritual life. It's not so much what a person has nor what they are that counts. Christ is not just a new guy in town; He is my Lord. Christ is not just another name; He is the Name above every other name. I now look at life in a new way.

We need to change our perspective if we are going to possess love like Paul where we are motivated by this love. We must do all that we can do to make God look good; we must look at things from a spiritual perspective in order to experience newness. Newness comes to those who have met Christ. For anyone who is in Christ is a new creation. Many of us feel that we are not becoming new, but the reason could be that we are not looking at life from God's perspective. We still see life through the human perspective. We are not motivated by love. We are not doing things to the glory of God. We are not seeing things spiritually. Therefore, we are not feeding the new person with the food necessary for us to function in a new way. The newness will not be evident unless the force in our lives agrees with the new person whom each of us has become.

The butterfly is encased in a caterpillar cocoon. It is there all the time. A butterfly is not made, it's evolved and so there comes a time when the butterfly breaks loose. It breaks the restraints that the caterpillar has put on it and begins to fly. Such is the case with the Christian. We have been made brand new, but we are encased in old flesh. The "caterpillar" of this old flesh tries to keep the "butterfly" of our new creation housed up. The cocoon of our humanity tries to keep the butterfly of our spiritual being from flying loose. So we are hung up in the "old me" rather than breaking forth to become new.

CHAPTER IV

THE POWER OF TRUE LOVE

And David spake to the men that stood by him, saying, What shall be done to the man that killeth this Philistine, and taketh away the reproach from Israel? for who is this uncircumcised Philistine, that he should defy the armies of the living God?

And the people answered him after this manner, saying, So shall it be done to the man that killeth him.

And Eliab his eldest brother heard when he spake unto the men; and Eliab's anger was kindled against David, and he said, Why camest thou down hither? and with whom hast thou left those few sheep in the wilderness? I know thy pride, and the naughtiness of thine heart; for thou art come down that thou mightest see the battle.

And David said, What have I now done? Is there not a cause?

And he turned from him toward another, and spake after the same manner: and the people answered him again after the former manner.

And when the words were heard which David spake, they rehearsed them before Saul: and he sent for him.

And David said to Saul, Let no man's heart fail because of him; thy servant will go and fight with this Philistine.

And Saul said to David, Thou art not able to go against this Philistine to fight with him: for thou art but a youth, and he a man of war from his youth.

**And David said unto Saul, Thy servant kept his
father's sheep, and there came a lion, and a bear,
and took a lamb out of the flock:**

**And I went out after him, and smote him, and
delivered it out of his mouth: and when he arose
against me, I caught him by his beard, and smote
him, and slew him.**

**Thy servant slew both the lion and the bear: and
this uncircumcised Philistine shall be as one of them,
seeing he hath defied the armies of the living God.**

**David said moreover, The LORD that delivered me
out of the paw of the lion, and out of the paw of the
bear, he will deliver me out of the hand of this
Philistine. And Saul said unto David, Go, and the
LORD be with thee.**
I Samuel 17:26-37

We have been attempting over the last few chapters to
explain the elements, rewards, direction and perspective of love.
I have explained that commitment gets us peripheral results. But
if we want to experience heaven and earth and God's deepest
activity in our lives, we have to be for real. An authentic Christian
is one who is not playing games but is willing to face Christian
reality.

So let's discuss that aspect of true love as it pertains to
power: the ability to be supernatural in the natural realm; the
ability to operate on planet earth with the authority of heaven at
our disposal. There are two extremes when we talk about power.
One extreme is to say we don't have any power today like they had
in the Old Testament because that was for back then, not for us
today. God was involved back then, and today we are more of a
spiritual group, and we cannot expect that kind of power. Paul
said, "I want to know the power that got him out of the grave,
power that makes a dead man walk again. I want that power!" The

question is why don't Christians have power? Is power available? Why are we so powerless?

The other extreme is to want God to execute His power the same way He used to execute it. God has the same power He had in the Old Testament. God does not always use His power the same way. God's method may change but He is and has always been a God of power. The question is how do we, as God's children, develop God's power? It goes back to the level of our commitment. Most of us are committed to that which we see. If we can see it, understand it, touch it, or taste it, then we believe we have power. But, generally speaking, if what we do is limited to our five senses then another human being can do that too. The thing that makes us different is that we have the power of God at our disposal. One of the great stories that shows what true love looks like when it garrisons the power of God is found in the book of I Samuel. The players are well known. A giant named Goliath and a kid named David. This is more than a narrative event that we tell our children. One of the tragedies of reading the Old Testament is that most of these stories never get through to the core of our hearts. One of the things we need to do with our children is to make sure the lessons we teach them are more than just good storytelling.

Paul says in I Corinthians 10 these things were written so New Testament Christians could understand in illustrative form what God's power looks like. Therefore, God's power is still operative although we may use different methods. The Israelites and Philistines did not get along very well together. They would rather fight than live together. Whenever they were together there was a potential war. Israel had one up on the Philistines. They had won the last battle because God had helped them by opening up the ground and inducing an earthquake. But the Philistines decided that it was not over yet. They came back together for another battle. Only this time, they had another strategy. On this occasion both sides decided they did not want to lose a lot of men. One of the customs of the day was when there were two opposing nations, a particular representative would be selected of each nation to fight on behalf of his nation. The victory of the representative would be transferred to the nation— so, if your rep won it meant that your nation won— but if your rep lost then your nation lost. It was a way of saving lives.

That is the situation. From behind the line comes a man called Goliath— he comes out and calls for their champion (in verse four). Goliath is from Gath and stands 9'9". He is huge. He is dressed to kill— bronze helmet, scale armor, bronze shield. This man is dressed in 120 lbs. of gear and possessed plenty years of experience in battle. Here is the giant Israel had never seen before. Israel was God's people. The Philistines did not belong to the people of God. Let's see what God's people did in response to this monster man. Verse 11 says that when Saul and all the people heard what Goliath had planned to do to Israel, they were dismayed and greatly afraid, scared, terrified. Who was terrified? Saul. Remember when the people selected Saul to be king, one of the reasons they chose him was that he stood a shoulder above all the people. He was a man's man and the people's champion. When Saul saw Goliath, he threw in the towel and decided not to be Israel's champion any more. All of Israel responded in the same way because they did not have a representative to match the enemy.

I can bet that so many of us are facing some Goliaths at 9'9 in our lives today— situations and circumstances that are confronting you and no matter how big you are, you are saying no way, I can't do it. The thing in front of you has you afraid. It may be that relationship that you cannot make up your mind about; that marriage you can't get together; that financial situation which seems so overwhelming; and you say "how can I take on this Goliath?" Have you felt that you are facing the pressures of life and the pressures of life are talking to you, saying "I dare you to solve this problem?" The scene shifts in verse 12. It says David (whose father told him to take some food to his brothers on the front line) leaves his sheep, and went to the battle line where his brothers were fighting. Israel and the Philistines come to face each other and just as he arrives, in verse 23, Goliath shows up again. No volunteer wanted to fight him. He came out, spoke the same words and David heard him. The question is what did David hear that got him mad? David heard Goliath and he heard something the other men did not hear. Verse 24 says that other men ran when they heard Goliath, for they were greatly afraid. But see what David heard: in verse 26 David gives the first aspect to power. David spoke, saying what will be done for the man who kills this Philistine? For who is this Philistine who taunts the armies of the living God? The problem was all that Israel saw was Goliath. David says now wait a minute, this man is uncircumcised, meaning he has no covenant with God's people. God had gone into covenant with the circumcised nation. God is in agreement with us. This joker is 9'9"— how tall is God?!

You only have power when you are able to measure the size of your God to the size of your problems. If you do not learn to take the yardstick of faith and measure the size of your God against the size of your problem, your problem will always be bigger than you can handle. Remember Paul's philosophy of life: no matter what state I am in I can be content because I can do all things through Christ who strengthens me. What Paul had come to discover was to measure the size of his God to the size of his problem. Now the problem is that most people will say "my God is big, so big you can't get over him, so wide you can't get around him, so low that you can't get below him." They will talk that talk, but the issue is how big is your God measured against the size of your problem? Not, how big is your God because you are in church and He is supposed to be big. He is supposed to be big on Sundays. The important thing is to look at how big He is measured against your problems. The question of how powerful we are can only be measured when something challenges our power. If you have a Goliath in front of you, that is an opportunity to shine. Until we learn to measure God against our problems, we will always be on the losing side. How do we hold on to the faith when it seems like the enemy has won? If we haven't learned to hold on then we don't understand this thing we call power. David says God is alive. Israel should have known that. They probably had devotion that morning, saying we should learn to trust God. They walked out the door and there was Goliath, 9'9" and they neglected to apply what they learned about God in front of the problem. Personally, the reason I want to take on the giant called mathematics, and the giant of van driving for cash is that I want to put God in front of a financial problem. We must say, "God, you are alive." Notice the shift in verses 26-27. The brother of David asked why did you come down, and with whom have you left the sheep? His anger burned against David. He was saying to David, "I know you. You love to talk about what you can do; always walking around the house being positive. I know your insolence." This is nothing new for David. He always wanted to do something unique and now he seemed to be up to no good. In verse 32, David said to Saul "let no man's heart fail on account of him. Your servant will go out and fight." In other words, don't sweat it— I have it all taken care of. David had confidence. Everything is wrong with confidence that totally rests in you. But everything is right with confidence that realizes that God is bigger than your problem. This biblical thinking says there is no problem so great that your God is not greater. As Corrie Ten Boom puts it, "there's no pit so deep that God is not deeper still." If we can realize this, then we have a basis for positive thinking. One of the reasons Christians don't feel power is when the human resources are gone they give up, they quit. Saul says to David there is a problem: you are a youth. This man has been a warrior from his youth, and he is a grown man. He's got all the experience and you have none. Saul was saying to David, logically this is a dumb decision— completely insane. There are many times you realize that to do what God says makes people say you've got to be crazy. I know people will tell you don't do it. Don't apply God's principles to that problem because it doesn't appear logical. Have you measured the size of your God against the size of your problems? If we see only what our eyes tell us we would never be supernatural Christians. That's why Elijah was so great when he looked out his window at the people who were coming to kill him. Elijah said don't worry about it. Elijah stayed around the house where angels with swords of fire were. He saw something. Those of us who know God see something. He saw beyond that which is seeable, just as we see— a living God.

David had an experience with God before which made him realize that God could come through for him. He knew the giant was in trouble. Let me tell you what most of us do: we run into a problem and if we have not used God in the small problems— when we are facing the big problems we are not likely to use Him then either. Or, we may want to use Him but don't know how. The key is to let God work where we are, so when we get out there and don't know how to swim on our own— we have had a track record with God. David gives a history lesson on God. To all parents, that is why the Bible says to tell your children what God has done, to take this history of God with you. However, the tragedy is that parents are not giving their children any history of God to take because they haven't embraced the living God, and therefore they cannot transfer anything. David said I have a resume, a history to display. One day I was out there with a lion and a bear came, and the lion caught a baby lamb. I went after the lion saying "You may be king of the jungle but you're not taking a lamb of mine!" David attacked the lion and took the lamb out of its mouth. And when the lion rose up against him, he seized it by its beard and struck it to kill it. Your servant has killed both the lion and a bear. This Philistine will be like one of them, since he taunted the armies of the living God. Is your God alive, or is God a cross which you wear around your neck? a picture hanging on a wall? a Bible covered in dust from underusage? Is your God a building on the street, or is God the living reality of your life? If He is this— the living reality of your life— then you should act like it. He is a powerful God.

What was the basis of David's power? The basis was that David believed God was alive, and he was defending the reputation of God. The thing that makes God open up heaven for us is when we make God look good. If we are telling God "I want You to get the glory," God says, "you need some power." That is why Moses could get God to change His mind. God said "I will wipe out the Israelites," but Moses says "God, don't do it because the nations will make fun of You." The Bible says "and God changed His mind." We can pray to change God's mind only if God will look good. In verse 39, Saul put his armor on David but David could not walk because he had not tested them. So, David took it off. Verse 40 says David chose five smooth stones from the brook. Goliath had four brothers, and David was going to take on the whole family because they were messing with God.

Believing God doesn't mean that you do nothing. Trusting God does not mean that you sit there and God does everything. Trusting God means we do what we can and that which we can't do we surrender to God and let Him do the miraculous with it. God gave us abilities so that we can use them for His glory. He wants to use our power. We must always connect faith with obedience. David used what he had and confronted Goliath. Goliath said, "Am I a dog that you should bring a stick to me? Don't be a grasshopper, so I can give your body to the birds." David said (to the giant) you look impressive but I came to you in the name of God. Though the giant cursed him David knew the Lord would deliver the giant into his hand. That took a lot of faith. David says the reason he is fighting the giant is so that God may get the glory.

In verse 47, the fact of the matter is there is a God in heaven. If we are going to make a difference in our communities (especially in the inner cities), our aim should be for people to know that there is a God. It is God's method which works. So David decided to do it God's way. David ran towards the giant with the first stone and knocked the Philistine out.

God used the skill of David best. However, we tend to want God to try to use junk, leftovers. David gave God his best and when the stone hit the giant, God drove it in. The Bible says it sunk and Goliath fell. The Bible says David prevailed. What is your Goliath that you're facing today?

29

CHAPTER V

REMEMBERING GOD

And thou shalt remember all the way which the LORD thy God led thee these forty years in the wilderness, to humble thee, and to prove thee, to know what was in thine heart, whether thou wouldest keep his commandments, or no.

And he humbled thee, and suffered thee to hunger, and fed thee with manna, which thou knewest not, neither did thy fathers know; that he might make thee know that man doth not live by bread only, but by every word that proceedeth out of the mouth of the LORD doth man live.

Thy raiment waxed not old upon thee, neither did thy foot swell, these forty years.

Thou shalt also consider in thine heart, that, as a man chasteneth his son, so the LORD thy God chasteneth thee.
Deuteronomy 8:2-5

The great story of the Old Testament is the story of God's people and their movement from slavery to freedom. It is the great movement of Israel leaving Egypt on their way to Canaan and the tour that got them through the wilderness. Much of the books of the Old Testament deal with that movement. From a biblical perspective the wilderness was a necessary institute. It was crucial that God's people go through the wilderness. It was no mistake that there was the dried up, non-productive slice of territory before they received the blessings of Canaan.

Israel had become so miserable that they knew they couldn't stay there any longer. Canaan had looked so beautiful that they knew that's where they wanted to go. The purpose of the wilderness was to prepare them to get there. The purpose of the wilderness was to let God's people see God on their way to Canaan. The reason why God established the wilderness journey is quite clear. God knew there would be the possibility for His people to forget Him. He knows that we have this great ability to pray to Him on Monday because we need Him to come through for us and to forget by Saturday that we ever needed Him on Monday. As Israel desperately needed Him in Egypt, the Bible says they waited and cried and begged the Lord for deliverance and the Lord heard their cry. The Bible said God came down and spoke to Pharoah saying "Let my people go." When they got on the other side of the Red Sea, they sang and shouted and prayed. God knew if they could go directly from Egypt to Canaan— without the wilderness they would miss the reality that God sets us free, that we might enjoy Him and our freedom. If they had gone directly into Canaan from Egypt they would have immediately seen the land flowing with milk and honey and start to enjoy God's benefits without realizing who God is. The wilderness was designed to teach them about God so that when they arrived in Canaan they would not only enjoy the benefits of God but would also enjoy the person of God.

We find in Deuteronomy 8 God's people on the verge of entering the land of Canaan. They had been wandering for forty years in the wilderness. They were going in circles because what should have lasted a short time took forty years. There was an extreme condition of unreadiness proven. That's another characteristic of the wilderness. It proves they were not ready for Canaan. They wanted Canaan but didn't want God. God never delivers us from Egypt to get to Canaan with Him still in the wilderness. We have this potential to thank God one day for what He has done and forget Him the next day like He never did it. When we sit at our banquet table and enjoy the benefits, God says, "I have a problem with that."

They were on the verge of entering into the land. They had gone around in circles; the older generation died off, while the younger generation was on their way to entering in. The older generation could not enter the promise land. They could not go in because they did not learn the lesson of the wilderness. The wilderness after Egypt is necessary. That is why James, chapter 1, suggests you count it all joy when you go through the wilderness of your life. The wilderness is necessary before you can receive the crown of life because God can always come through for us and give us the tranquillity we desire; therefore, we must perform in the wilderness. Moses, in this chapter begins to tell the Israelites everything God has said, to follow the commandments so that you might live. For God there is a direct relationship between obedience and living. By living, God does not mean physically existing, because the Israelites were alive for forty years. But they were alive going in circles. We know people like that where their hearts are pumping but their lives are going in circles. They go from one bad situation to another, one bad relationship to another, one depression to another because they have not yet learned to live.

And thou shalt remember all the way which the LORD thy God led thee these forty years in the wilderness, to humble thee, and to prove thee, to know what was in thine heart, whether thou wouldest keep his commandments, or no.

Who fed thee in the wilderness with manna, which thy fathers knew not, that he might humble thee, and that he might prove thee, to do thee good at thy latter end;
Deuteronomy 8:2, 16

Now God explains why the wilderness was important in Verses 2 and 16. God said I lead you through the wilderness for two reasons: 1) To humble you, and 2) to test you. If our desire is to get to the place in our lives where our lives are pleasing the Lord and where we are actually living for the Lord, I can assure you that on our way there we will run into enough things to later humble us or test us As you and I live our lives in this world, there will be enough trials, continuous difficulties, dry spots in life, those spots that are exciting, those days that are difficult days, and those years we describe as the worse years of our lives. There is no way around the wilderness. There was no way for Israel to leave Egypt to reach Canaan and bypass the wilderness. They had to go through the wilderness.

If you name the Name of Christ, I have bad news and good news for you. The bad news is that we will go through the wilderness when we live for God; we will run into those periods when life closes in on us. He says during those periods, this is a relationship morally readjusting to a new lifestyle since you met Christ. You pray and God has not yet delivered you. You remain in this wilderness situation and God has not provided you rest. Rest is the promised land. The Bible calls Canaan rest— which is deliverance from the wilderness to enjoy the benefits of God's blessings. We go through our wilderness for God to humble us and test us. To be humbled means to be put in a situation where you have to have God. Unless God comes through, we are in trouble. I don't care how successful we become, and how much we accumulate there will be times in our lives whereby if God does not intervene we are in trouble. We will not make it. There is sickness that money cannot buy a cure for, tragedy where all the knowledge of who you know cannot resolve. There are times when God puts us in situations whereby unless He comes through, there would be no solution.

There is only one way for us know whether we trust God. It is easy to trust God when there is no need. To trust God is easy when you can pay cash, use American Express, Visa or MasterCard. It is easy to trust God when you know where tomorrow's meal is coming from. We must go to India— where their prayer "give us this day our daily bread," means that literally. Yet when we ask for daily bread what we mean is Lord make sure the daily bread that is already in my cupboard and has been there several days does not give me cancer. So what God will do is place us in a position in this world to try our faith in God. A place that will prove if we really TRUST Him! Why? Because God never made Canaan for us to enjoy it, while we leave Him in the wilderness.

What God does not want is for us to enjoy all the beauty that He has made without knowing the Maker. So what God does is hold the solution to our needs, and He allows us to experience a wilderness season first to test us. How long do we have to go through the Wilderness? Answer: Until we get the message. But what we have is a unique ability to get ourselves out of our own wilderness season. We say, "I don't have to take this." We can at times take ourselves out of our wilderness. But I have news for you, there will be another wilderness around the corner, because the message is to walk humble with your God— trust in your Lord. Until those two lessons are learned, there is no end to the wilderness. That is why they wandered for forty years.

Verse 3 describes that humility wherein He (God) lets you experience hunger. It was God's idea that your stomach hurt. If there is any lesson we in contemporary society have not yet learned is that man does not live by bread alone. Jesus says, "I let you get hungry in the wilderness." Why? So that I might feed you. Why? So that you will learn that man not only lives by the bread he takes, but also by the Person who gives that bread. Most of us really don't believe that what we have is a gift from God. The bread on our table is God's gift. We assume that what we enjoy is our inevitable right to have it. In Verse 16, there is a contrast. He said I am going to allow a depression to take place as you go through the wilderness just to let you know that you not only live by bread but also you live by whether or not I provide it. We are here today not only because we have access to products that will keep us alive, we are here also because God makes the provision. God says if I am removed from the scene the bread is in trouble. How does He keep us remembering? God will keep us in the wilderness until we get the message. The sooner we get the message, the sooner we get out. Fighting God in the wilderness is a waste of time. God wants to teach us to be humble and how to depend on Him and He wants to expose where our commitment really lies. So He reminds them in Verse 4 of His provision that their clothing did not wear out, or their feet did not swell over these forty years. He wanted them to know that the only way they can explain the survival in the wilderness is because God took care of them.   You have walked around for 40 years in the same clothes— that sounds impossible— but God protected the stitches. There was no store in the wilderness to buy from. As they grew, their clothing became elastic and grew.

When I look at my own life, I have no human explanation of how I made it. In college and graduate school, I did not have any money during my educational experience. There were two realities. I was a humble man because I needed divine provision. I needed God to come through and I can't remember how many times I went to the mailbox and there was $5, $10 as He carried me through. God said I sent you through the wilderness and you were hungry, that I might provide manna. So when you get to Canaan and are satisfied when you have more than enough money and food, you will remember how you made it through the wilderness.

We all have to remind our children that we have been in the wilderness, and they will also go through it. We try to make their wilderness short in training by providing for them. However, some of us are still in the wilderness not because God wants us to be there, but because we have not decided to leave. Also, because we have decided not to be humble before God. We decided not to place our dependency on Him. God knows that our milk and honey is flowing, but He doesn't want that to stop us from trusting Him. Then Verse 5 suggests that God will discipline us like a father does his child. By discipline He doesn't mean punish, but provide guidelines for training. Any good parent allows their children to hear them say no in order to prevent an overabundance of permissiveness. If a child gets a yes every time they have a want, the Bible says we are not loving them, rather we are destroying them. Parents say no to allow their children to go without so that he/she can be wholesome and not become a spoiled brat. God says you need the wilderness because I don't want you to enjoy Canaan and leave Me outside.

So verse 6 suggests that God is bringing us all into divine blessings. There is good out there for our lives. God is taking us somewhere, but He will not deliver us to where He is taking us until we learn to walk humble with our God and depend on Him. Verse 10 gives us an exhortation: when you have eaten and become satisfied, you shall bless God, beware lest you forget God. God says after you are satisfied, remember your God. What God wants us to know is that our stomach is only full because God filled it. How do we remember God? By saying grace, yes, but that's not all.

God says you remember Me by <u>Obedience</u>. We can pray as much as we want, but if we do not obey Him, God says we have forgotten Him. If our obedience does not reflect our remembering, then we do not remember our Lord. We have Christians who say grace all the time, but whom God has no say over their lives. Remembering God is living in obedience to His reign over our lives. So God concludes this in Verse 12. Our church is filled with success stories about people who have bought homes and moved from apartments. However, it is possible that before we had the apartment, God had more of us. He got more of our time, energy and our obedience. But now we have been blessed, we have forgotten that the house, education, and job are gifts from God.

We forget that we do not climb the ladder by bread alone, but by God's provision. Now the house, job, cars, and furniture keep us from Him, which is exactly what God did not want. Look at how many of you have five coats and ten suits. Now you moved from 10 to 50 dresses. The silver and gold has multiplied. There is an IRA, CD, checking, and multiple stocks. God says lest when you have accumulated all the things, your heart becomes proud. The higher we climb the ladder of God's blessings, the more humble we should be. The more we have been blessed, the more we should worship God. But the tragedy is the more we have been blessed, the more we have forgotten our God. When we didn't have much, we loved to come to worship because that was all we had. Church was a priority because we didn't have competition, but now it's the last thing on the agenda.

Verse 19 says it shall come to pass that if we forget God, we shall perish. What that is saying to us is that if all we have comes from God, and we then go and enjoy God's blessing without dealing with God's person, He will treat us like He treats the non-believer. How does He treat non-believers without obligation? There is no rest in this life. You may be successful, yet still in the wilderness. Rich and miserable, educated but no wisdom, houses but no home, because we have forgotten our God did not bless us so we could forget Him. He blessed us so we could remember Him.

Will you remember your God today? Will you give priority to God? At one time, no one knew your name, but now people know your name— because God is with you. Humbly walk before your God because the sooner you do, the sooner you will leave the wilderness.

CHAPTER VI

REWARDS OF TRUE LOVE

But I rejoiced in the Lord greatly, that now at the last your care of me hath flourished again; wherein ye were also careful, but ye lacked opportunity.

Not that I speak in respect of want: for I have learned, in whatsoever state I am, therewith to be content.

I know both how to be abased, and I know how to abound: every where and in all things I am instructed both to be full and to be hungry, both to abound and to suffer need.

I can do all things through Christ which strengtheneth me.

Notwithstanding ye have well done, that ye did communicate with my affliction.

Now ye Philippians know also, that in the beginning of the gospel, when I departed from Macedonia, no church communicated with me as concerning giving and receiving, but ye only.

For even in Thessalonica ye sent once and again unto my necessity.

Not because I desire a gift: but I desire fruit that may abound to your account.

But I have all, and abound: I am full, having received of Epaphroditus the things which were sent from you, an odour of a sweet smell, a sacrifice acceptable, wellpleasing to God.

**But my God shall supply all your need according to
his riches in glory by Christ Jesus.**
Philippians 4:10-19

Paul tells us that when we commit to loving God it carries with it a voluminous amount of rewards. When we unreservedly place at HIS disposal all that we are, all we are about, and all that we possess, it becomes available to the Christ and manifests in rewards. Two of those rewards are given in Philippians, chapter 4, which is one of the most powerful passages in the New Testament written by one of the most prolific Christians named Paul the Apostle.

In order for us to understand these verses we have to know where Paul is. He is in jail. He is in prison waiting to see what the decision will be if he should live or die after Caesar decides. He is incarcerated, all alone and had been made a mockery of by preachers. So Paul was alone and nobody knew where he was. It is that man who is writing: no friends anymore; by himself; and under the penalty of death.

So he says in verse 10, I rejoice in the Lord greatly. When was the last time you have been able to say that in bad times? When things were going wrong there was a well bubbling inside where you rejoiced. Generally, when it is a sad time not only do we not rejoice, but everyone who comes in contact with us knows we are not rejoicing. Paul writes this letter saying "I am happy today because of the church's concern" for him. Paul was poor, hungry and the church had come to his side. Then comes those precious words, let's not miss them: "I do not speak for want. Do not send more money because I have learned something. I have learned to be content in whatever circumstances I am. I know how to get along on humble means and prosperity. In every circumstance I have learned the secret of being filled and going hungry." Paul says I have learned the secret called contentment. Contentment means you are satisfied on the inside regardless of circumstances on the outside. So many people do not have that.

One of the rewards of a committed life is contentment. If you have not yet gained contentment you ought not look for it because it is through commitment that you truly gain contentment. I hope we realize that we live in a world grasping for contentment. People want this satisfaction but don't know how to find it. They are striving to find this thing called contentment.

For many of us, when the money is rolling in, things are content. When bills are paid, things are content; a lot of friends, things are content; good health, things are content. But, if you take away the money, friends, good health, and home— all of a sudden they go into a depression and the contentment is gone. That is because we live in a world where people do not understand where to find contentment. So what we do is get in the rat-race of the world order, trying to find what the world has not found— contentment.

The reason Madison Avenue is doing big bucks is because we are not content. They understand that all they have to do is keep something new on the market. They know we are never satisfied. All they do is come up with a new product and call it new and improved because they understand when new and improved is placed beside what we just bought, we are not content, not satisfied. John D. Rockefeller when asked "how much does it take to be content?" answered, "one dollar more." We are not content, we've just got to keep going, keep after it because people are not content.

The tragedy is many Christians are in the same bind. They are saying, "I love you, Jesus, but I'm not content." They are always frustrated, always mad, always upset, always torn on the inside and they are never satisfied.

There is a story of a king who was looking for contentment and was told by one of his astrologists that he could be cured for his lack of contentment if he could find a contented person in all of his kingdom. So they searched the kingdom to find such a man, to take his shirt back to the king and the king would be cured. After they searched long and hard, the contented man was found in the kingdom but he did not own a shirt.

What we have to understand is, the essence of contentment is not what we have or who we know, or where we work. Some of us go to work looking for contentment and have not found it. You have tried numerous relationships and have not found contentment. You have accumulated possessions such as a house, car, furniture, and you thought these things would be the solution but what you didn't understand is that you can have a house but no home. You can have a spouse but not a marriage, because contentment is a secret. If you want to know whether or not you are content, you can only test this not by the good times, but by what you are like in the bad times. Contentment must be measured when things are going wrong, not when things are going right.

Andre C. says "How will I know he can solve them if I never had a problem?" Anybody can say in the good times "I trust in the Lord," but the proof of the pudding is when we are called upon to depend on Him. That is the essence of trust. So Paul says contentment is a secret. The world is looking for contentment, not knowing it is a secret. (Sssh, don't tell anyone. It's not available to everyone.) It is not possessed by every Christian. It is a secret, Paul says, that I have learned whether I'm in prison waiting to die, or whether I'm in prosperity. The money is rolling in, but it really doesn't matter. It is good to be concerned, but that does not control whether we are content. What is the secret? The answer: "I can do all things through Christ who strengthens me." That is the secret. You may have responded in your head but unless it has left an indelible impression inscribed on your heart, we don't know it. Here is true positive thinking, "I can."

What Paul is saying is that these things which belong to Christ that I'm instructed on regarding our lives, all these things Christ has told me to be. I can do and be all of those things because God provides us the enablement to be and to know. So there is nothing that God expects that I can't do because God takes it upon Himself to provide the power to pull it off. The reason most of us are not content is because we do not have the power. We don't have the authority to be what God wants us to be and do. The secret of contentment is where we have such a dynamic relationship with Jesus Christ where I have become preoccupied with Him so that in my preoccupation with Him He takes personal responsibility to enable me to be and do all He has called me to be and do. The reason most people are not content is that they are trying to become so by themselves. Paul says that is not the secret. "I am so preoccupied with Christ," so He takes the responsibility of enabling me to be and do all He has called me to be and do.

The reason we fail in our Christian life is we are not preoccupied with Christ. To put it simply, we are preoccupied with this world order. Why do you think the psychologist tells us we are not able to think of two things at the same time? One thing must go when you think of the other. You can't think of number one and number seven simultaneously. We can think of them in sequence, but not simultaneously. That is what Christians want to do, to mix them. We can't mix air and water. If you have air in the bottle and put water in, the air will have to come out. You must have one or the other. What Christians want to do is to have both at the same time. Paul says the reason we never have supernatural power and strength and therefore can never be satisfied is that we always have to get one dollar more, one more possession, as the goal of life.

Paul is not condemning things, because he says he knows how to live in prosperity. He is saying it will never provide contentment, only preoccupation with Christ can do that. How preoccupied was Paul with Christ? Let's take a quick tour:

For to me to live is Christ, and to die is gain.
Philippians 1:21

For me to live is Christ and to die is better. When I get up in the morning it's Christ. If you want to know what's on my mind at lunch time, it is Christ. In the evening time, it is Christ. I close out my day with Christ. I dream about Christ. The first words in the morning from my lips are "Good morning, Lord." Did that mean he didn't deal with business? No, but he wanted to know Christ. How do I infuse You in business? When he talks about politics, Christ was right there. Christ was the center of his life. That is why his life was so exciting, because he had infused Christ in every part of his life.

Look not every man on his own things, but every man also on the things of others.
Philippians 2:4

"Don't look out for yourselves but have this attitude that was also in Christ Jesus." He says think like Christ. Have Christ's mind in you, so that we act out Christ in our daily lives.

But what things were gain to me, those I counted loss for Christ.
Philippians 3:7

"Whatever things were gained to me those things I have committed as loss for the sake of Christ. It was Christ who was the motivating factor of his life. In verse 10, that I might know Him and the power of His resurrection and fellowship in His suffering. Do you see his heart and what made him tick? Chapter 4, verse 4, "Rejoice in the Lord always and, again I say, rejoice." He is consumed by Christ. If we are not consumed with Christ, we will never find contentment. That is the secret. Madison Avenue will not flash that on the television screen and say that all those who are miserable, come be preoccupied with Christ. That won't sell. That is why it's hard to convince Christians to be preoccupied with Christ. You say you don't know how hard my situation is, but it couldn't be worse than Paul's: Nero is about to cut his head off, and he is saying, "Rejoice in the Lord." Most of us rejoice in the bank account, in the house, car, clothing, but there is no contentment there. Then he says, "I can do all things through Christ." How can you do it, Paul? Christ was his enabling power to pull off a contented life. Let's look at some words with "I can." Christians love to say "I can't." I have a problem with that if it is something God says you can. Those are two words Christians have no business using, if it is something God says you can. If it is something God has not talked about, then you are right about saying you can't. If you say you can't fly with your two hands, you are right. God never told you that you could fly. So, we can only use the two words to apply to what God says we can't do. But, if God says you can do it, you can do it.

God told Moses, "Tell Pharoah to let my people go." Moses said, "I can't. I stutter." God looked at Moses and got mad: "Moses, who made your mouth to speak and ears to hear? What do you mean you can't. I told you that you can." If I made your mouth what is the problem?" Moses was told to throw that stick down and it became a snake. Therefore, you can, maybe you won't, but we can because God says we can.

"I can do all things." The reason we do not live miraculous lives is we believe the world order. You can't live that way. You cannot live a pure life in this world. You cannot be honest. You cannot break this habit. YOU CAN! For you became a new creation, so tell the old body "I will not live this way any more." Notice this did not happen overnight. Paul said that he *has learned.* It is not our strength. We are right to say that we can't on our own, but we can if we are preoccupied with Christ. As we are preoccupied, Jesus does His thing in us and then we can.

Listen, if you put Michelangelo from the grave in my body there is no sculpture I could not create. If you resurrect Bach and put him in my body, there is no piano I could not play. Resurrect Muhammed Ali and there will be no person I couldn't whip. Put Babe Ruth in this body, and there is no homerun I could not hit. What I am saying is, if you resurrect Jesus Christ and put Him in your life, there is nothing you cannot do. It is His life taking up residence in our lives, empowering us to do the impossible. I can because Christ can. We have to ask, can Christ? Then we ask, does Christ want me to do this; then what's the problem? The only reason I can't is because I am not hooked up to Christ, because if I am hooked up, then I can.

That is a marvelous promise. We can kick that habit, heal that relationship, deal with that depressed mind. But we have to be preoccupied with Christ. Satan desires for us to get preoccupied with our problems and stop talking about Christ.

There is a second reward: **"and my God shall supply all your needs according to His riches in Christ Jesus."** First— My God. Which God is my God? Yahweh of the Old Testament. What did He do? He spoke and the world came into existence. My God spoke and waters separated from dry land. The breath of His mouth brought the animal kingdom into being. My God. He spoke and man got shaped into the marvelous creature that he is. My God is the One that let rain fall for forty days and nights. My God was with Joshua when he fought the battle of Jericho. My God shall supply everything you need. There is no need that you have that My God doesn't have the ability to supply. Whether your need be financial, physical, emotional, social, etc.— if you need it, My God will take care of it.

When you look at the need, you may say "I don't need what is happening in my life right now." Well, it all depends on who is defining the need. I took my daughter Aisha to the doctor's office for an immunization. She saw the needle and said, "I don't need that." But I told her "This needle will prevent you from some disease which you might have down the line." From the way she fought, she did not agree with my explanation. Her statement was "I don't need that." I had to help hold her down. I did that because I knew something she did not know. She needed that shot.

Not only does God supply the need of delivering us out of problems, He supplies the need by putting us in the right kinds of problems to develop us to be the right kind of persons we should be. In both cases of being delivered or developed, He is still meeting a need.

How does He meet the need? According to His riches in Christ Jesus. When God meets our need He does not do it out of His riches, but according to His riches. There is a big difference because if you say you need ten dollars, out of my money I give you ten dollars and would have that much less because I gave you out of my resources. God does not have that problem. I can be depleted; whereas God can never experience that. He comes along with our need and He evaluates each need and provides all the supply necessary to cover the need and has no less. If you came to me too often for ten dollars, we would have a problem. But we never have that problem with God, because God's resources never run dry. He never has less because He has provided for us in the past.

If God supplies all my needs, how come I am not having all my needs met? If further questions include: "what about my depressed mind? I prayed about it. My sickness? Nothing happened." What most people don't understand is this is a conditional promise, not unconditional. An unconditional promise is one that God makes regardless. A conditional promise means there are conditions we must meet in order for God to satisfy the promise. What did Paul say to the church? "You have done what God told you because you gave for the building of God's church; you have sacrificed living for God's glory; you made God number one in your life, bringing people to Christ— because you have done what God has told you to do. Paul had good news for them: My God shall supply all your needs."

The promise is only to those Christians who are doing God's thing. God is tired of being ripped off without any commitment from His people. God is no fool. I can imagine God is saying heaven is available to you. I will not keep giving you blank checks. I will only give you checks for you to write off my account. When you have a need, I'll check your account to see if you have made any deposits to cover your checking account. Can God cash your check, or is your account empty?

God has the ability to meet needs but He is no fool to cash a check against an empty account. Our personal banks don't do it, so why should God?

If we have met the conditions in verses 14-18, He is obligated in verse 19. We like to run to God in emergencies after we have not worked with Him all year; we have not served Him all year; we have not sacrificed for Him all year; we have not made His goals our goals; but now we say "Lord, I need You like I have never needed You." God says I am not a bellboy or Santa Claus. He is our Lord, the Manager of the House.

You say you don't need anything? If you just keep living, you will need God sooner than you think. What does your account look like? Are you getting the benefits of your account on earth? One reason I feel confident about our future is we have been doing God's thing, which is winning people to Christ. We have been doing all we can to serve people and ministering to the needs of the poor.

I've heard of an interesting way in which zoologists catch monkeys. They place a jar containing small pebbles on the ground to attract the monkey to the pebbles in the glass. The monkey will squeeze his hand into the jar and grasp the pebbles, but because he is dumb, he does not know that he cannot get his closed fist with the pebbles out of the jar. Those pebbles have become his reason for living and he's holding on to them. He doesn't understand that as long as he holds on to the pebbles, he will never be free. It will hold him as a slave. That is the way many Christians have become as they reach into this world order for pebbles. It will be these very same pebbles that they thought would save them that will actually hold them captive. I see it every day where Christians are caught in materialism and immorality, etc. People start taking a little alcohol or a little drugs, and then they are caught. These people usually start with little habits and now they say "I can't get my hand out." No longer do they control the pebbles, but the pebbles control them. God says "Let the pebbles go and be free because when I put pebbles in your glass they won't trap you, you will enjoy them under Me."

CHAPTER VII

THE SACRIFICE OF TRUE LOVE

And it came to pass, that, as they went in the way, a certain man said unto him, Lord, I will follow thee whithersoever thou goest.

And Jesus said unto him, Foxes have holes, and birds of the air have nests; but the Son of man hath not where to lay his head.

And he said unto another, Follow me. But he said, Lord, suffer me first to go and bury my father.

Jesus said unto him, Let the dead bury their dead: but go thou and preach the kingdom of God.

And another also said, Lord, I will follow thee; but let me first go bid them farewell, which are at home at my house.

And Jesus said unto him, No man, having put his hand to the plow, and looking back, is fit for the kingdom of God.

Luke 9:57-62

In God's awesome love for us, He will never tell us just the good without the bad. As a matter of fact, He will tell us both sides so that we will know the whole story. Satan is not like that. Satan will tell us half the story. When we drive down the highway, there is a poster of a man with a glass of Jack Daniels in one hand and a woman on the other, dressed in a three-piece suit with a smile on his face, suggesting that he has made it. The impression is that if you know how to handle your Jack Daniels, you will know how to handle your lady. Satan will tell us about that side, but he will never show a picture of a man who started on Jack Daniels and has not been able to stop, nor will he show photographs of families that have been destroyed. Satan never shows the disaster.

This is also true in the church. We come and everyone looks good but if we could look behind the scenes, we would see the rest of the story. One of the things we are exposed to in the ministry is seeing the other side of people. We see beyond the Sunday dress or suit, and we get to see people where they live and hurt. Jesus is unique in that He tells us what the other side is like. He does not tiptoe, but makes us aware that there are demands and that a commitment is needed.

I have discussed in another section the rewards of true love. We stated that one of the rewards is contentment. Paul declared "in no matter what state I am, I can be content." One of the blessings of knowing Christ and walking with Christ is the knowledge of being content, of not letting circumstances dictate our attitudes or our success. Then we saw that there is another reward of commitment, having undeserving guarantee of having our needs met. "My God shall supply all your needs according to His riches in Christ Jesus." The Lord says, I will take care of your needs because you shall have a bank account in heaven that is full. Since your account is full, because you prioritize Me, when you need Me I will meet your needs, whether those needs are mental, emotional, spiritual or social.

The reason many Christians don't get their needs met is that their spiritual bank account is empty. They have made no investment in heaven but want heaven to make an investment in them. How many times have we seen people get spiritual when tragedy strikes because they desperately seek God's assistance. God says the first thing He does is to check our account to see how much of heaven has been deposited therein.

This is the good side, but there is also a downside to true love. I need to tell the whole story. It is erroneous to tell a non-Christian that if you accept Christ all your problems will be solved.

If you become a Christian you will be president of the "company." Everybody will love you and seek out your advice.   If we tell this tale we will be talking about heaven, not the reality of life on earth. I need to serve notice that there is a downside to true love. In Luke 9 we are told of the sacrifice it takes to love God. Take Jesus, for example. He had been rejected even on His way to Calvary. If we were in Jesus' company, we would have been mesmerized by what He could do. Just by the snap of His finger, He could make a blind man see and the lame man walk. By the bowing of His head in prayer, 5,000 men were fed by a couple of fish and pancake loaves. But what the people did not see was that while Jesus loved to, was capable of, and wanted to do all those things, He was heading to a place called Calvary. He was on His way to die. It is easy to lose sight of that because we tend to concentrate on the fringe benefits. It is possible to become consumed by the benefits of Christ without realizing the cost.

Let's examine some of the costs in this passage. In Luke 9, verse 57, one man says "I will follow you wherever you go." That sounds good, many of us have said that before. "Lord, just tell me where you want me to go and I will go. Inform me of what you want me to be, and I will become it." We make these glorious promises to God. It may be after a sermon you have heard, or a song that brought tears to your eyes because at the moment you were deeply sincere and you wanted to go all the way. Jesus says many people make that commitment without understanding what they are saying. The case illustrated here says that Jesus responded to this man by saying "The foxes have holes and birds have nests, but the Son of Man has no where to lay his head." Jesus wanted this man to realize that He was not sure where He would sleep. He said "I can show you a fox and he can show you his home. I can show you a bird and he can direct you to his home. But do you understand that when you travel with Me, you may have to give up some comforts?   Your plans may have to change.   Do you understand that commitment to Me means you are not tied into the security of this world order?"

There is a prosperity philosophy that is around today. It goes like this: "I'm the King's kid. The King owns everything and since I'm His kid, He wants me to own everything. Therefore, I put on a success mentality that says God wants me to be a millionaire." There is a problem with that thinking because it suggests that anyone who does not reach that goal is outside the will of God.

Jesus is not saying that to be committed to Him means go sell your house, find a cubby hole and live miserably. On the contrary, Jesus suggests that commitment means, if need be, if requested, we are available to become insecure for His sake. Commitment to Christ means that sometimes we have to make choices. In certain instances, these choices may go against economic security. We should be willing to give up the bigger house or finances in favor of Christ.

If Job were living today, based on the economics of this passage, he would be living in a ten-bedroom house on twenty thousand square feet of land. Yet despite this, Job was in the will of God. The Lord provided everything for him. Then one day he got the tragic news that Wall Street had taken a plunge and he was now a pauper. Job responded by saying, "Praise the Lord." Despite the death of his children and the painful diseases inflicted on his body he said, "Praise the Lord." You ask the question, "Job, what's wrong with you? You have lost your home, and children and you say Praise the Lord?"

Job's statement is the underlying assumption of what Jesus told the man in Luke 9. Job said you don't understand that the Lord giveth and the Lord taketh, so blessed be the Name of the Lord. What Job is saying is I can only lose it because God gave it. How can we get mad at God for taking anything because without God I never would have enjoyed such pleasures for this long. That is difficult for us to understand. We believe that if God gives us something, we have the right to it as long as we live. We forget the condition given in 1 Timothy 6 which reads "Naked you were born and naked you will die." Therefore, everything between birth and death is a gift.

God demands a commitment from us which He is at liberty to test, so that as we follow Him, He can call us to trade in anything of value. If He calls me to a life that does not have the security that I am used to, I will be ready. Jesus is serving notice that He has the right to be Lord. We who are living in this culture today have more than Christ ever had. Very few of us will ever be called on to offer a whole life sacrifice whether by going to the mission field or by selling our earthly possessions for God's sake. Few of us will ever have to give up the security that we are accustomed to, so we should be even more thankful and committed because God has allowed us to enjoy more blessings for a longer amount of time. Yet we do just the opposite. We get so accustomed to enjoying the blessings and benefits of the privileges of life: good health, clothes, homes, and cars, etc. We become so afraid that Jesus might ask us for it, that we stay away from Him. We do not want Him bothering the gifts He gave us, that same blessing which He demanded to be Lord over. The very things God has given us to enjoy strangle us as we leave Him out, and we become a slave to these pleasures rather than allowing God's blessing to lift us to a higher level. Whatever God has given us, whether it be homes, a car, or clothes, enjoy them to the glory of God but always in a detached manner. In this way, if/when God calls us to move on, we will not allow these blessings to become a hindrance to our commitment made to follow Him.

There was another man who came to Jesus and he took the initiative: "I will follow you," he says. Jesus knew this guy did not understand what he was saying, but he had potential. Jesus says, "Follow Me." The man responded "I will follow, but I've got something to do first. Let me go bury Dad. I will be right back." That does not seem like a difficult request. All he wanted was the opportunity to bury his father. There is only one problem: his father is not dead. It was the custom of the day that the older child stayed home and took care of the affairs of the house until the father dies. Then upon his father's death he would receive the inheritance and move on to the priorities in his own life. This man was saying as soon as Mom and Dad die, then I will get around to being committed to You. This sounds like us: "Jesus, I will live for You as soon as I buy this new house, when the children grow up, when my career is over, when I get out of school." We procrastinate all the time. "Lord, I will follow you but on my time table, my schedule, my program. When Daddy dies, I will give You all my life. I'm not ready yet." Jesus counterattacks this with "What do you mean you are not ready yet?" Whenever we say we are not ready, we are assuming that we will be around to get ready. That's not normally what happens. The longer we live the more encumbrances we gather. It is always more responsibilities, bigger businesses, and life becomes more complex. It seems later never really comes.

If we are going to make an impact for God, it is because we have stopped putting God on the waiting list. So Jesus responds in verse 60 "Let the dead bury their own dead, but as for you go and proclaim the kingdom everywhere." Jesus told this man that he should be a proclaimer of life. There are people back home who are spiritually dead, and dead persons are taken care of by death. You have met the Savior and have become alive, so don't get caught up in death. Experience life.

Do you know that if you accept Christ in your life, you will never die? Paul says from the moment our breath stops, we open our eyes in the presence of God. We don't need to fear death because Christ declares "O death, where is your sting. O' grave where is your victory?" The sting of death is sin, but sin has been conquered by the blood of Christ and since sin has been destroyed we can live by the blood of Christ. Furthermore, since death has no sting and Christ has caused that which did sting to die, then what we are about is life. We are alive and shall never die. That is why when a Christian dies it is a celebration because that believer has been ushered into the presence of the Lord. Since Christ declares that we are alive, we ought to do what living beings do. We have a message of life and we need to tell it. Let dead people take care of dead things, for you who are alive should go proclaim this life.

Then there is a third man who declares that "I will follow you, Lord, but permit me to say goodbye to those at home." That is not an inconceivable request. "Let me say goodbye to mother, father, sister, brother, uncles, cousins, and I will follow you." Let us understand the culture in which this occurs. In this culture, parties went on for ten days. So when he goes home, he would not be back to catch up with Jesus for many days. "After the party is over, I will follow you, Jesus." But Jesus says no one after putting his hand to the plow and looks back is fit for God's kingdom. There are no exceptions to this mandate. When you hold a plow it is imperative that you go straight ahead so the lines won't be crooked for the planting of your seeds. Jesus says, "Sir, once you make a decision for me, don't delay it." Jesus declares it difficult to plow with our hands going in two different directions. God says it is impossible to be His people when we are being torn in two directions.

That is what happened to the children in Israel. Every time they looked back, Egypt looked better than Canaan. They saw all of God's miracles but they still wanted to return to Egypt. The reason we have so many dissatisfied Christians is because they haven't looked forward where the plow is. They keep looking back to the world. They cannot develop consistency, and Jesus says we are no good for the Kingdom that way. God told Lot to tell his family upon leaving Sodom and Gomorrah, "Don't look back because I will be doing things I do not want them to see." But Lot's wife, with that temptation to go backward, looked and she became a pillar of salt and was henceforth good for nothing.

Many Christians are like that. Every time it looks as if they can make a mark for God, they look back. God can't use them anymore. When we look back it is hard to start going forward again. If you exercise, the worst thing you can do is to take time off because the body easily becomes unaccustomed to the function and performance. What Jesus is saying is forget the party. You've got to march on if you are going to do My work. One person put it this way:

> I count dollars while God counts crosses.
> I count gains while God counts losses.
> I count by worth by things gained and stored,
> But He sized me up by the scars that I bore.
> I coveted honors and sought degrees;
> He wept as He counted the hours on my knees.
> I never knew until one day by the grade how vain
>   are the things we spent life to save,
> I did not know until my loved one went above,
> Richer is he who is rich in God's love.

Do you know anything of value that cost you something? Whether it was your schooling or business, it cost you something to accomplish it. As one missionary said, he is no fool who gives up that which he cannot keep to gain that which he cannot lose. God is calling us to sacrifice our lives. As the song says, "I have decided to follow Jesus, no turning back." The problem they say with living sacrifices is that they keep crawling off the altar. Someone asked a violinist how she became so accomplished and her reply was "it was planned neglect." She neglected everything that was not related to her goal. God wants you to have planned neglect where God becomes your only goal. God wants to be number one. You need to stop playing double games. You have to be committed to serve God as He deserves to be served. But everything starts with a personal decision. God is tired of the excuses. He wants your life.

CHAPTER VIII

SEEKING GOD

A Psalm of David, when he was in the wilderness of Judah.

O God, thou art my God; early will I seek thee: my soul thirsteth for thee, my flesh longeth for thee in a dry and thirsty land, where no water is;

To see thy power and thy glory, so as I have seen thee in the sanctuary.

Because thy lovingkindness is better than life, my lips shall praise thee.

Thus will I bless thee while I live: I will lift up my hands in thy name.

My soul shall be satisfied as with marrow and fatness; and my mouth shall praise thee with joyful lips:

When I remember thee upon my bed, and meditate on thee in the night watches.

Because thou hast been my help, therefore in the shadow of thy wings will I rejoice.

My soul followeth hard after thee: thy right hand upholdeth me.

But those that seek my soul, to destroy it, shall go into the lower parts of the earth.

They shall fall by the sword: they shall be a portion for foxes.

**But the king shall rejoice in God; every one that
sweareth by him shall glory: but the mouth of them
that speak lies shall be stopped.**
Psalm 63:1-11

There are persons today who are groping in the wilderness
of life. People struggling in what David called a dry and weary
land. That is, you are in a stage of your life where emptiness has
taken up occupancy even though you call yourself a child of God.
There are those periods of ruts that we experience in life, which
encompass us so thoroughly that no matter where we look, there is
nothing but desert. Perhaps your desert is related to your marital
status. As a married person you don't seem able to get it together,
and you are caught in the wilderness of that frustration. Perhaps
you are single and have not found happiness and fulfillment. In
fact, you hate to hear the word single and that has become a desert
for you. Could it be that your desert is the eight hours of work on
that job which you now find it burdensome to get up for in the
morning, knowing that you have to spend a major portion of your
time in a place you find intolerable? For others, they are in a
financial desert or an emotional and social desert. What does one
do when faced with the reality of finding oneself caught in the rut
of life? Some of us are in the wilderness because we messed up.
We made a mistake and now we are paying for it, and it doesn't
seem that the price tag will ever be completed.

Psalm 63 is a passage for people in the desert in which the
further you walk the more tired you get, and all you see is expanse
of oasis. David had a word because of a major portion of his life
in a desert. There are two occasions which David spent in the
spiritual desert. One of his desert experiences was because of
righteousness. He was running for his life from Saul who saw him
as a threat to his throne, and in order to get rid of him, Saul lost his
sanity and sought to kill David. So David had to run to the desert
of Judah. The other occasion was because of sin. Bathsheba came
into his life and he committed adultery. His son turned against him
and wanted to kill him and that sent him into the desert. The

reality is that when you are in the desert, you are facing a major challenge. When this happens sometimes you say, "Lord, why me? What am I doing in the desert?" Other times we know why we are in the desert for it is crystal clear. But this Psalm is for desert folks, no matter how we got there.

Notice what we call the superscription, that is, the statement above the Psalm. It says a Psalm of David when he was in the Wilderness of Judah. This superscription gives the context about what drew the Psalm out. One of the reasons why the Psalm has a special ring is because it comes out of experience. They are born in existential situations. The real life circumstances that produced this David did not compromise the Psalms from his library. They came because he and God were living together in a real world with real people having real problems. It is in the Psalm we can see that in spite of David's mistake, God could look at him and say "that man David is a man after My own heart." What was it about David that captured God's attention? The good news is no matter what mistakes we have made, God can reach beyond that and love us— mistakes that have never left us, mistakes as single parents, the desert of child rearing and the burden that comes with living with the mistake that someone else made.

David has a word from God. Here we have in verse 1 the beginning of the development of his argument. David's argument is simply this: it is in seeking God that one finds spiritual confidence during the rough times of life. It is when one passionately pursues God during the rough points in life, that one is enabled to develop spiritual confidence. The inner working of your being begins to shift when one has pursued God during those rough times. Let me summarize what David is not saying. He does not say that seeking God automatically guarantees the immediate reversal of circumstances. He does not say that. What he says is that seeking God produces spiritual confidence when you are in the desert until you find an exit from it. The reason David was called a man after God's own heart is because of verse one. He knew where to run. The songwriter sings that song,

"Where do I run when there is no one to talk to? Who do I lean on when no one wants to listen? Is there a refuge in the time of tribulation? " Then she answers the question, "I go to the Rock of my salvation, the stone the builders rejected. When life all around is sinking sand, on Christ the solid Rock I stand." I know He is able. I go to the Rock. Where do you turn when all of a sudden you seem to be in the desert? David says, "Oh God, thou art my God and I seek you earnestly." Psalm 63 can be divided in two parts, verses 1-5 where David is seeking God during the tough times, and verses 6-11 where we find David gaining spiritual confidence after having sought God during the rough times.

So the first five verses tell what it means to seek God. Verse 1 says that seeking God means you go after Him earnestly. Seeking God is not just going to church, or saying our prayers before going to bed. That is good and necessary, but when David talks about seeking God he means more than a few minutes given to God at the end of the day. When you are in the desert, you just don't need a shot of water you need a jug of water. A token of water won't do: you need a fountain hook-up to a dam. He said, "I seek you earnestly. My goal, my desire to reach You goes to the soul." He said, "My soul is dried up and needs water." David said that his entire being craves for God, and it is not until our entire being seeks God that we do it earnestly. Seeking God earnestly suggests there is no competition between television and being with Him, or between radio and God. When we are going after God earnestly, everything else takes second place.

When we are hurting, our focus is on solving that pain and our seeking God takes on another dimension. It goes deeper, and all the TV shows like "Living Single," "All My Children," "America's Most Wanted" become meaningless. That is simply because seeking God in the desert is most pressing. One of the things the Bible teaches consistently and ongoing is that God only feeds hungry people. If we are not hungry, He won't feed us. Why cook for somebody who is already full? It is a waste of time. But wherever you see the great men and women of the Bible, they are hungry people. Jesus put it this way, "Blessed are they who hunger and thirst after righteousness." Why? Because they will be filled. Those are the only people God feeds.

The reason why there are unfulfilled Christians is that they are not very hungry or hungry for the wrong thing. Remember when God revealed Himself to Moses, and Moses said "show me more of thyself" (Exodus 33:13) that I might know thee. He got a little bit of God and he said that is not enough. What a little of bit of God does, if you are hungry, is to make you more hungry. One of the problems with dieting is tasting. The person says I am just going to taste this and the problem is usually all the things you want to taste are fattening like ice cream, cake, pastries. The problem is once you taste it, you have excited the taste buds and turned them on. Having turned them on they become disappointed if you stop. That is what happens when we seek God. David, Moses, and Paul wanted more of God. Paul declared, "that I might know him and the power of the resurrection." Paul says I am willing to pay any price, even suffering, to know the power that raised Him up from the dead. That became the passion of his life.

David also suggests even in his mistake and failure that he wanted to know God. So the first thing about seeking God, if we are going to know Him, is that we have to go after Him. That is how most relationships develop. One person may decide that he is not going to let this person reject him, so he persists. It is in the steadfast pursuit that one attains knowledge. The reason why in the wilderness of life God allows us to be in a situation is that our genuine desire is reflected in the dedication of pursuit. We know we are serious about God when we pursue him at all costs. No matter how dry the land is or how far away God seems. David said, "I'm thirsty." That's exactly what happened to Jacob. He said to the angel, "I am not going to let you go until you bless me." His thigh bone was disconnected and put him in more pain and he said, "Let me go." The angel did not want to go. What the angel really wanted to know from Jacob was how bad do you really want Him? Jacob said "I will not let go until you bless me." This is an example of an appetite.

Notice in Psalm 63, verses 2 and 3 there is also remembrance if we are going to seek God. David said I saw You in the sanctuary. David remembered His work and the excitement and enthusiasm from the testimonies and saw what God was doing. He had a reason to praise God. He said now I'm in the desert, but I remember the excitement of being in the sanctuary. The reason we should be pursuing God during the good times is so that when the bad times come, we have something to remember. If we don't have a history with God in the good times, when all the bills are paid, when relationships are strong, children well behaved— and if we don't maximize those times— when we get to the desert, then we won't have anything to remember, and therefore we won't be sure of what to lean on. It is being in the sanctuary, David says, that allows you to see His power and glory. The miracles are the times that He brought healing to others, provided finances for every situation and encouraged all those needing encouragement. You look back and say. "I remember that because of what has been etched in my memory from experiences. You are confident that He will be water in a desert. He said, "thy lovingkindness is better than life." What he remembers is God's character. He knows that God cares for him.

It is lonely in the desert. We feel like nobody understands or cares, but David said he remembers God's lovingkindness, that He has made a covenant with me to love me regardless. David closes this section by saying to seek God means to give Him praise. "I will bless you at all times and as long as I live." I hope we never wait for a praise service to praise God. We get lifted up when we praise God and what praise does is change our focus. Why is it necessary to change focus? Because when I am in the wilderness, the only person out there is me. The focus is on my misery, my problem, my marriage, my singleness, my children, my job, my lack of funds. Yet, what the Lord says through David is the desert is the time we pray not for what our problems are, but we praise Him for who He is. Why? Because it changes our focus. As a man thinketh, so is he. Remember, it is how problems are viewed that becomes more important than the problems themselves. What you believe is what you think. Therefore, if you think wrong, you will act wrong. So what people do is enter into wrong relationships because they think wrong. Yet, what praise does is affect our thinking. It allows us to reflect on God's greatness, His creation, His power. As you acknowledge God's person, work and worth and then return to your problem, all of a sudden the problem takes on a different dimension. The problem may remain, but you have a new perspective. In our prayers there must be praise, bringing to mind who God is. In verse 5, he said my soul is satisfied. Remember in verse 1 "my soul thirsts," but now in verse 5 he says my soul is beginning to be satisfied. That leads him to the second half of the psalm where seeking God produces spiritual confidence.

He says when I remember Thee I meditated on You at night. Have you ever been awakened with God on your mind, just contemplating Him? One of my desires— with all that is going on: the speaking engagements, the growth in our fellowship and the expanding ministry— is to slow down enough to enjoy and meditate on Thee. Our grandparents used to roll God over in their minds and that gave them inner satisfaction, which enabled them to handle the outward problems. David says I meditate because He has been my help. He is changing my attitude.

Has the Lord helped you before? Do you remember times when you said I can't take it anymore and all of a sudden on eagles' wings you came out? After David prayed, the Holy Spirit gave him more to remember. The reason many of us don't remember is we don't slow down enough to meet with God. As he praised God he obtained wings to fly above his problems. When he said what he had done, verse 8 suggests I am not going anywhere. My soul cleaves to Thee. I like it right here. I have found joy, purpose, peace, right here. Why? Because Thy right hand upholds me. The right represents power and strength. God is holding us. My son Darius has a way when we are walking of asking me to hold his hand. Once he said, "Hold me, Dad," and I said, "I've got you." But he insisted, "No, I am holding you. You should hold me." What he wanted was more than feeling my hand. He wanted the security of the grip. Comparatively, notice David's new confidence as he suggests that those, even those who seek his life, shall be destroyed, but the kings will rejoice in God. To this God says He will take care of his problem and will take care of him. You may think this is so old-fashioned and is not relevant to us, but look at verse 11: everyone who swears by Him will glory. This is not just a privilege of the day, it is a privilege for you and me.

This is why if you are struggling in the desert, there is a way where the worship of God gives confidence. You cannot make it until the wilderness ends. If your struggle is financial, social, or a personal battle (a habit that is destructive) there is a confidence that God can meet you there. Let us summarize the entire Psalm for it says that seeking God brings confidence during the tough times. I know you are going through a tough time, but just saying that repetitively will not help. We have to go to the Rock, for simply complaining how hard life is doesn't change a thing. Some people love to complain because their joy in life is complaining about how bad things are and how rough it is. Don't misunderstand. The job of the church is to help those going through the rough times. My question, however, is what are we going to do? We can't do like the world does. When things are rough for them, they go out and find things to make it rougher. They call it fun, only to find out further on that, all it comes down to is what you sow, you will pay for now or later.

What should we do when we have to seek Him? To seek Him we must first learn from Him and commune with Him.

CHAPTER IX

A TRUE MODEL OF LOVE

If there be therefore any consolation in Christ, if any comfort of love, if any fellowship of the Spirit, if any bowels and mercies,

Fulfil ye my joy, that ye be likeminded, having the same love, being of one accord, of one mind.

Let nothing be done through strife or vainglory; but in lowliness of mind let each esteem other better than themselves.

Look not every man on his own things, but every man also on the things of others.

Let this mind be in you, which was also in Christ Jesus:

Who, being in the form of God, thought it not robbery to be equal with God:

But made himself of no reputation, and took upon him the form of a servant, and was made in the likeness of men:

And being found in fashion as a man, he humbled himself, and became obedient unto death, even the death of the cross.

Wherefore God also hath highly exalted him, and given him a name which is above every name:

That at the name of Jesus every knee should bow, of things in heaven, and things in earth, and things under the earth;

**And that every tongue should confess that Jesus
Christ is Lord, to the glory of God the Father.
Philippians 2:1-11**

Paul begins Philippians 2 by saying that one's private communication with God always manifests itself through the way one treats the saints. If there is no relationship with the saints, there is limited relationship with the Lord. It is in the horizontal relationship that we demonstrate vertical reality. If our way of life does not demonstrate a meaningful, caring, sharing oneness between brothers and sisters in Christ, then there will be a weakened witness of Christ's love and fellowship of the Spirit.

When Paul speaks of that spirit, he examines it from the standpoint of a dynamic relationship with the Christ. It is to the degree we possess this dynamic relationship that this kind of spirit of sharing, caring, and oneness pervades our existence. The church should be caring because Jesus has consistently cared for us. We should be caring people because Christ has consistently ministered to us. Paul having introduced this wanted to present Christ as a model of how Christians ought to think. Paul is after our minds. He wants to teach us how to renew our minds, so he introduces the model in verse five by saying "have this attitude in yourselves that was also in Christ Jesus." He admonishes us to learn to think like Christ.

Paul says the Christian has to have a different kind of mind, learning to think divinely. One of the worst statements a Christian can make is "but everybody else is doing it." A major struggle in the Christian life is to continually allow the Spirit to guide our actions, as opposed to letting this world order have active influence. We are constantly inundated by mass media telling us how to think and what we ought to think about. Therefore, our judgment of most things depends on how the world reacts. It is amazing how many times Christians say things in the same manner as the world, sadly indicating that there is no renewal of their minds. Paul says we need to learn to think like Jesus.

Now, the question becomes how does Jesus think? What is the model which we should follow? Paul first identifies who Jesus is. In verse six he suggests that, although Jesus existed in the form of God, He did not regard His equality a thing to be grasped. The best way to paraphrase this is that Jesus did not believe His identification with God was something He had to hold on to at all cost. Jesus existed long ago in the form of God. Note that the word "form" spoke of a Roman stamp. When something was selected by the Roman government they would stamp it, and what came out on the paper was the exact image that was on the stamp. Paul says this is what Jesus is like. Jesus existed in eternity as the exact duplicate of who and what God is. So when we talk about Christ we are not talking about someone less than God but someone who is identical to the duplicate of God.

The question is, what did the plan to present Christ as a model look like? First of all, Jesus in the God form had at His disposal all the conveniences of glory and none of the inconveniences of earth. His existence in the form of God, thus equality with God, was not something He felt was at risk when the need came up for man's salvation. He had no fear of leaving His sovereign position in order to come down to earth to meet our need— even though (in our frame of thought) it would have inconvenienced Him. Therefore, when the plan was developed that somebody had to come down to earth to provide salvation for us, Christ did not say "I'm sorry. I am not about to leave heaven to go down to those miserable people on earth to provide them salvation!" Rather, He said "I'm not so much into being God up here that I cannot become human down there. I'm not so much into glory up here that I cannot help people down there." If Jesus thought He had to maintain divinity in order to protect His Godness from anything assuming His position and, therefore, stayed in heaven, we would be in trouble. Because if there were to be no Savior, there would be no salvation. If there is no salvation, there would be no hope. And if there is no hope, we would have nothing to look forward to for eternity. But Jesus said "I am ready to leave glory and come down to earth simply because there is a need."

What point is Paul making as he instructs us to learn to think like Christ? What mindset is he talking about? A mindset that knows who you are but doesn't let who you are stop you from ministering to somebody else who has a need. We have this idea that comes from the world that we have to protect what we have. Jesus says if I protected what I have, you would not have anything to protect. When we know who we are in Christ, we know we will never lose it by ministering to one another's need. Jesus did not stop being God when He became human. Jesus was still God after He became human. The difference is that He now encased His divinity in humanity to meet human needs.

Many people like to brag about who they are and what they have, but God's response is that our possessions are only important when we use them for someone else. God says who we are only happened because He made us this way. He allows us to become so we can help somebody who has not yet become. We can therefore demonstrate the mindset of Christ, which was illustrated when He gave up heaven and came down to be our Savior. He did not hold on to His equality. Verse 7 suggests that He emptied Himself and became a slave in order to be made in the likeness of men. God could have said "I love you down there." And man's response would be "So what! I'm in trouble," because in our time of need verbal love is in vain if action is not taken to confirm the love and meet the need. For example, if I fall in a ditch and you say "I care and want you to get out of that ditch," but I'm still down here and you're up there caring— that does not help me. Obviously, I need you to do something.

What did Christ empty Himself of? Did He empty Himself of God and become human? No. The question is not what did He empty Himself of, but it is what did He empty Himself into? He did not empty out God and pour in man. He emptied all of God into man. He did not stop being God and leave His divinity in heaven. Jesus did not give us the leftovers. He poured all of God into us so that we could have all of God. What He did was take all of divinity and pour it into man, so now man can become more than man. So man can become what man could not be before: God/man. God is now being poured down into man, making us what He always intended us to be. There is nothing that belongs to God that we did not get when Jesus emptied Himself into us. That is why He was some kind of person because God is some kind of God. That is why the life of Christ is a life extraordinary. He emptied Himself, pouring all of His deity into a purpose to help humanity. So when you look at the grace and blessings of God in your life, the question becomes— So what difference does it make that God has done this for you? So what if God has blessed you with great abilities? So what if you possess superior intellect? So what if God has healed your body? How has that impacted the purposes of God in this world? If what God has done for us does not aid us in serving others, His purpose would not be realized because serving others is the mindset of Christ.

Jesus saw our need and came to do something about it. Jesus set aside His riches and came in the form of a bond servant. How rich was Christ? He was very wealthy, for the Bible says by Him everything that was made was made. Everything, according to Scripture, is at the disposal of Jesus Christ. He gave up that wealth and the enjoyment of glory and became a bond servant.

A bond servant in the Greek is *doulos*— a slave. This term was used of the Roman slaves who were the most abused, misused, ill-treated people of their day. One could not get lower on the scale than a *doulos.* It is amazing that Jesus Christ, the King of Kings and Lord of Lords, was born of poor parents, in a stable with dirty animals, wrapped in dead people's clothes, born of poor parents and lived in virtual poverty all of His life.

Jesus owned everything but He set it aside because He wanted to give us a mindset. This is the mindset: no matter how rich you are in terms of resources, intellect or talents, all of your riches should have the element of service. Service is willingness to go so low that you want to go to the bottom of the barrel for someone else. Christ came and was born a *doulos* because He wanted to identify with the bottom of the barrel. Therefore, Christians should never say "I'm too good to identify with that person or those people." The most need-oriented people ought to be Christians because we should be able to make our resources available all the way to the bottom of the barrel.

Philippians 2, verse 8 suggests that Jesus was found in the appearance of a man. In perfect love for His Father, He humbled Himself to look like us, and in obedience He accepted His calling as Savior of the world. If we had walked with Christ on earth, we would have found something phenomenal. He would always say He had come to do someone else's work. He would always say why He was here. When asked, "Jesus, what are you doing?" He replied, "Carrying out My Father's work." Jesus would make it clear that the reason He came was so that God would be written on every page of His life. That is why He humbled Himself. Why did He have to humble Himself? Because nobody could make Him do it. Furthermore, the need was greater than His divine right to exist in heaven, so He gladly gave up His right. He could have called ten thousand angels with the snap of His finger while on the Cross, but He humbled Himself. Jesus said there was a need out there and I must meet it.

The Bible tells us to humble ourselves under the mighty hand of God. In other words, the more we are blessed, the more humble we should be. The reason God has a problem with blessing us is because we have this thing turned around. The more we have, the higher our shoulders go and the higher our heads are raised. We don't allow His blessing to produce more humility but rather more pride. That is why the Bible talks about the seven great sins which God hates, and pride is at the top of the list. For what pride says is that we have pulled ourselves up by our own bootstraps. What God says is "I put the boots on you, and you are to look at My blessings as a way of thinking which says you have been, so you can make a difference among My people."

How much did Christ humble Himself? He humbled Himself in obedience to the point of death. To humble oneself to die in another person's place is ultimate humility, which requires the capacity of sacrificial love. God did not ask Him to have cardiac arrest, a pulmonary condition or even a stroke, but Christ was to humble himself to die the death of a criminal on the Cross. Jesus did not just die. He had to die after being carved up piece by piece. He was given the Roman scourging which was administered by a whip that lifted out parts of His flesh. This left Him with massive holes in His back, which explains why He could not carry the cross up the hill. The splintered wood was digging into the holes in His back. He was God. He made the wood that built the cross, and yet He had to carry it. If we had seen Him on that cross we would not desire Him. He was a bloody mess. They beat, bruised and insulted Him. They spit on Him and crowned Him with thorns while every bone in His body was out of joint. In evidence of His humanity, while experiencing immeasurable agony, He begged His Father to let this cup pass. He may have preferred another way to meet the need of sinful man. You can imagine that Jesus was not performing flips in heaven about going to earth to die for us, but He concluded "not My will but Thine be done."

Do you see the mindset? Christ said I have come to do Your will, and if that means the Cross so be it. This is what God has called on us to do, to follow the model of Christ. To take all that God has done for us and make it available to be used by Him. Our purpose is to get His mindset. This is a radiant love of the One who came and died for us.

CHAPTER X

TRUSTING GOD

Trust in the LORD with all thine heart; and lean not unto thine own understanding.

In all thy ways acknowledge him, and he shall direct thy paths.

Proverbs 3:5-6

Let's pretend that we are attending a funeral service and for the sake of argument, you are the one in the casket. We have just eulogized you, and now the door is open to the limousine and you are being transported to the cemetery. Hundreds of cars are lined up as your notoriety has swept throughout the country, and people have come to bid you farewell. We have arrived and the final prayer is said at the cemetery. The six-foot hole now awaits your casket. The tears of loved ones and friends run down their cheeks as they are saddened by your departure. Finally, you are laid to rest.

A few days later your tombstone arrives, and they are ready to set it. The question I have for you is "what would be written on it?" What would be the last statement you would leave behind that would articulate what your life was about? When the last word is recorded on the tombstone for the world to remember you, when family and friends visit your grave on Memorial Day, what would be the first and last thing they would see left behind? Would it read along the lines of:

He became the millionaire he always wanted to be
To a loving husband and father
To a loving wife and mother
To the business person of the year

If you could not write on your tombstone "a Success for God," you would not have lived all of your life to the fullest. No matter what accomplishments you have recorded on your tombstone, if it does not include that you did what God sent you here to do, then you would not have lived the life God intended for you. How would your tombstone read if it were placed over your grave today?

If I were to ask Paul the Apostle how his tombstone would have read, he probably would have said: "I have fought a good fight, I have kept the faith, I have finished my course. There is now laid up for me a crown of righteousness." Paul understood that he was put here for more than making a million dollars, or being a good father, good husband, wife, or business person of the year. He understood that he was on a course, a race, that was designed to take him to a particular goal. The question in life is: "Did I finish my course? Was I successful at what God sent me here to do?" At some point in your life you have said, I know I have been put here for a reason. The tragedy, however, is most of us go through life never finding the reason or even looking for it.

Two of the most precious verses about accomplishing a successful life under God are given to us in Proverbs. They are familiar verses which most of us quote: "Trust in the Lord with all thy heart and lean not to your own understanding. In all your ways acknowledge Him and He will make your path straight." The key is the last line: He will make your path straight. The word straight has to do with setting a course in life for us and guaranteeing that we will reach that goal. To someone on the path, God is letting you know that He is setting your path straight, designating your movement in life so that you arrive at the right goal, so you may accomplish what you were sent here to achieve. Make no mistake: we are here for a purpose. God has pre-ordained our presence on planet earth— you are not a mistake. The tragedy is if you live forty, fifty, or even seventy years and are still asking "why am I here?"

To understand these verses, we must understand the nature of Proverbs and the context in which these two verses are found. First of all, Proverbs are not promises. Proverbs are normative statements, axioms of life, whereby if we adhere to them, they are expected to work. They are normative expectations of following the prescription or advice of God. In the context of this verse, we have a series of couplets: series of verses, two at a time, that give internal or external blessings for an appropriate response to God. Couplet one, verses 1 and 2 "Do not forget my teaching" and "let your heart keep my commandments for length of days and long life will be added to you." If you do what I tell you, you will live longer. Couplet two, "Do not let kindness and truth leave you; do not become a cold-hearted person. Bind them on your heart" Why? So you will find favor and good respect in the sight of God and man. Do you want to be respected by God and man? Be nice. Verses 7 and 8: "Do not be wise in your own eyes" Don't think you have all the answers. It will be healing to your body and refreshment to your bones. You get physical health and strength listening to God and not the people on the corners who are going to lead you into the same mess they are in. The final couplet: "Honor the Lord from your wealth and from the firstfruits of your produce." Give Him from the top, not what is left over. Give Him...results. Your horn will be filled with plenty and your banks will overflow with wines. The way to get more is by giving more.

The couplet we want to look at today tells us how to be successful in life. The first portion of this is trust. The Hebrew word for trust is *Batad*. It means to lie down, to place the totality of one's weight upon that which is designed to hold us up. You trusted when you rested all your weight on your bed. You lay the totality of your weight on the mattress and spring, because you believed it had the ability to handle the weight. You trusted the bed because you had confidence in it. The word trust equals security, and we tend to find security in, lay down upon, rest on top of something. We all need to find rest in the Lord. A common mistake for many people is seeking success without trusting God.

Trust in the Lord is good for both heaven and earth. Trusting in God not only takes you up, it brings Him down. The reason we trust in God is because we know he can hold us. Everyone trusts something. Many of us fly and when we fly we are trusting many people. We trust the travel agents that they have made the proper arrangements concerning our flight destination. We are never introduced to the pilot nor do we get to check his credentials, yet we get on the plane believing that the pilot knows about flying. I rest the totality of my weight on the seat because I have trusted a number of people. God says rest the totality of your weight on Him. Rest everything on Him: success, failure, time. Trust: place all our weight on Him.

I heard a story of a man who was walking on a tightrope across the Niagara Falls. The crowd gathered to watch him. He had a wheel barrow, and on his second attempt across the Niagara he looked out and said, "How many of you believe I can carry this barrow across?" The crowd shouted "We believe you can do it. You have been walking the rope for years. We know you. We are aware of your ability. We know you won't fall!" He then asked, "Who then will get in the barrow?" Trust is not just verbal, but it is getting in the barrow of God. It is doing what God says to do, even when it doesn't seem to make sense. The reason many of our lives will crumble is that they are resting on the wrong thing. Homes will crumble because they are resting on the wrong thing. Our lives will crumble and children will crumble because they are resting on the wrong thing, instead of the Lord's commandments and promises.

How much should we trust the Lord? With all our heart—the inner component, the internal self. God doesn't want trust on our lips. He wants it from the inner depth of who we are. How do you know if your inner being trusts Him? By the way your legs move. The test for inner trust is external movement. If our legs are not moving, our hearts are not trusting. To trust in the Lord means that we believe He is worthy of total reliance. The first thing is to trust: to lay down on Him. Do not lean on our own understanding. It is okay for us to think as long as we don't rely solely on intellect. Whenever we think something, we need to check it out with God because our thoughts can be wrong. During counseling sessions when I tell persons what the Bible says, and they say "but I think..." they have decided to lean on their own understanding. God gave us a brain, and we are supposed to use it— to lean on His understanding, not ours.

Acknowledge Him. What does it mean to acknowledge God in our ways? It means not to give a token response to God. Acknowledge means awareness to operate our lives in such a way that we bring everything concerning our lives. It is to recognize His presence. Acknowledgment is asking God, "Do you have anything to say about what I am facing right now?"

We must make God an important part of our decision making. How do we know when we acknowledge God? There are two ways: 1) Our prayer life is one indicator. Paul says, "Pray without ceasing." In everything that comes up, bring God into it. We should have special times to pray, but things tend to happen often that are unexpected. We need God's attention all the time. Just as spouses say to each other: "Why didn't you check with me about that? I can't see how you made that decision without discussing it with me." God says "How can you organize and run your life like that without contacting Me?" We must pray about everything that comes up in our lives, and since things always arise, we will never stop praying.

CHAPTER XI

WORSHIPPING GOD

O come, let us sing unto the LORD: let us make a joyful noise to the rock of our salvation.

Let us come before his presence with thanksgiving, and make a joyful noise unto him with psalms.

For the LORD is a great God, and a great King above all gods.

In his hand are the deep places of the earth: the strength of the hills is his also.

The sea is his, and he made it: and his hands formed the dry land.

O come, let us worship and bow down: let us kneel before the LORD our maker.

For he is our God; and we are the people of his pasture, and the sheep of his hand. To day if ye will hear his voice,

Harden not your heart, as in the provocation, and as in the day of temptation in the wilderness:

When your fathers tempted me, proved me, and saw my work.

Forty years long was I grieved with this generation, and said, It is a people that do err in their heart, and they have not known my ways:

Unto whom I sware in my wrath that they should not enter into my rest.

Psalm 95:1-11

When people say they are going to worship God, usually what they are saying or ought to be saying is they are on their way to church. For others it means that they are going to sing some song that has the word "God" in it. The definition that people give for worship varies to a great extent which is contingent upon different factors. Some people enjoy exuberance from the service; other people would prefer a quiet service. However, the important issue here is what does God see when God looks at worship? Can we say that what we are about is in fact the worship of God?

There is a song that highlights worship. It is Psalm 95 which is a special Psalm. It gives us not only the content of worship but also gives the context of worship solidified by the proper mood and summarizes the worship experience. The Psalm can be divided into two halves: verse one to verse seven and verses eight to eleven. The first half gives us the call to worship. In these early verses God wants us to understand what He is looking forward to when we come and gather to collectively worship Him. The second portion reminds us that worship is not a game to be played. It is an exercise which requires serious participation. The Psalmist began his discussion with the imperative "O Come." Twice we are told to come. In the Old Testament there was no thought of staying in one's bed or sitting in front of the television with the idea of having church alone. In this Psalm the pilgrims journeyed to the house of the Lord. It was an exercise in which they got up and left their private place to join with all the others who agree that worshipping is a high priority in life. It is for everyone who recognizes that worship is not a request. It is a command.

This first passage tells us what we need to do when we come into the house of the Lord. We ought to sing for joy! God says when we come to His house, we should not drag in with low energy, but rather we are to come in with exciting exuberance in our hearts for an emotionally-packed worship. In worship, we should be filled with excitement, vigor and vitality. There is no such thing as the leftovers when we come to God's house. God says when we come we should ring out a song. In the early days this was done by a huge herald, a marching band going down the main street. Today, when we leave our houses, we should be entering a parade to join God's people in praising Him. God says there ought to be a collective excitement and enthusiasm because we are coming together with the people of God to worship. However, we don't do it that way.

In our culture today, Saturday night is the late night when people stay up until they run out of gas. Therefore, on Sunday it is hard to get up and rearing to go, so people drag into church and sit down with the excuse that "it's Sunday,"— as if it is okay to lose energy on that day. God says we miss the point. He says He requires the same energy in worship as we give to our favorite hobby or sporting event. God says He deserves the same excitement which we display at social functions. If you gather in your tuxedo to honor a dignitary with exuberance, then what about your God who created you and loves you? God raises the issue that worship should be exciting and meaningful. I was raised in a family who highlighted Sunday as the Lord's Day. Early in the morning we would be awakened by the singing of hymns or gospel music. The effect of this praise in music would bring us to an energetic high even before entering collective worship at the church. There was the idea that we are going to meet our God and join fellowship with the saints to glorify our God. There is room in worship for excitement. Worship ought not to be dull, rather it ought to be the most exciting period of your week.

Some people come to worship to hear the choir, and others come to hear the preacher. Still others come to look at the fashion show that takes place. But there is only one legitimate reason for coming to worship and that is for God to come to have an encounter with His people at a specific time. The reason why people do not hesitate to pay big bucks for material possessions or on sporting events is they see a value in such interests which are considered worthy of their attention. There will be exuberance and excitement because we have to make a value statement worth the expression of our energy. When God says come let us sing for joy, He is not asking us to mumble a few words. He says shout it out. Don't hum it if it is not to be hummed, but express it because this is for your God. It is wrong to come to church just in time for the sermon. He says we must come to sing. There is a misconception in worship that we are the audience and what we have come to do is to be entertained. We miss the point of worship if we consider it to be the Pastor's responsibility and the choir's responsibility to turn us on and to make us feel good for excitement. Worship takes place when God is the audience and we are turning Him on— where God sits and listens to His people express their love and praise to Him. The question we must ask is: Has God been made excited by hearing you sing, hearing the praise from your lips? Has God been turned on by your worship? Why worship Him like that?

Verse 2 suggests that He gives us a vertical and horizontal reason why we ought to be jumping for joy on our way to meet with God's people. The vertical reason is that God is responsible for the depths of the earth and the peak of the mountains. God controls way down low and way up high. There is nothing outside the sovereign control of God. This means that God has the whole world in His hand. If we like to get excited about a human being who can serve a touchdown or put the ball in a hoop, how come we cannot get excited about the God who made the earth upon which the touchdown has been scored? God says I have made the depths and the peaks and they are all under My control. God says that He is responsible for the sea and dry land that we have. We are either in water or on dry land. Everything exists in one of those places, so that no matter where we move we have the privilege. God says the reason we don't worship is that we forget that the water and land belong to Him, and He has the pattern on creation. The fact is that we have the privilege to get up and come together with God's people to express our gratitude. It is He who sees to it that we rise each day. So, God admonishes us to come with excitement and not sleepy-eyed and bent over— to come with exuberance and fire. You would be amazed at what it does. In order to produce fire, we've got to be able to see God. The bigger our God becomes, the more fire we have. Is it ever a wonder why people make choices about worship that they do not make about work? People stay home from worship when it is too hot or too cold, but they go to work without questioning the weather. Why? Because they have decided that being at work is of greater value than the inconvenience of being cold, and the decision is a value statement. The excitement should be about God and not about what we can make from life.

Then verse 6 gives another mood. The introduction suggests we come with excitement. Now, here He is saying let us bow down. In the first case it is exuberance. Here He wants reverence. There should be loud rejoicing but also sweet submission. Worship ought to have excitement where we clap our hands and shout "Amen!," but there are those times to be still. Worship ought to include a time when we cease from standing and go to kneeling, cease from shouting and go to pondering, times when we cease from exuberance and go into reverence. If all we did was shout Amen all the time, we would never hear what He has to say; or, if all we did was to bow our heads in reverence, we would be suppressing our natural emotions. We need worship to consist of both exuberance and reverence. God gives the reason that we should be filled with great anticipation that we are going to meet our Maker. We should be excited in God's greatness, for there is no one who can be compared with Him.

The thing that should cause us to be reverent is found in verse 7. "For He is our God and we are the people of His pasture and sheep of His hand." The reason we should bow our heads is that the great God of the universe has become our God. God is deserving of our praise because He is a great God. Yet, on the other hand, we need to ponder how could this great God become ours? He created everything but He loves each of us as if there were no one else around. When we met Christ He became ours and that should produce a great reflection on God. There is exciting worship when we realize He makes the seas and dry land.

However, this is magnified when we can praise Him realizing He is our very own. A God that big does not need us, but He decided to love us anyway.

Then the Psalmist moves from the call of worship to the warning of worship. The second half of verse 7 begins with the words "If today you hear His voice." We come to worship, shout and sing and even bow in reverence. God says let me inform you that I am not concerned with how you sing and how spiritual you look, but I'm concerned about the softness of the heart. When you hear God's voice there should be a change. Worship is designed for God to change us because we have been with God. If we come to worship and nothing changes, then we must have hardened our hearts. The more we worship and the less we change, the harder our hearts become. That is why we see people who come to church for fifty years and nothing about them ever changes. They may really love to sing and respond to worship, but nothing has ever changed. Their hearts calcify and become hardened and God cannot say anything to them. God gives an illustration of what it means to harden our hearts, and He gives the two locations of Massah and Meribah. The Psalmist is talking of two locations where God said these people are quarrelsome people and they test God. They witnessed God's parting the Red Sea and sending ten plagues on Egypt. God supplied them with meat and bread, and now they got thirsty. Before they trusted the God who opened the Red Sea; now they were complaining that they were a little thirsty. Instead of their thirst driving them to come to God, they complained against God for His deliverance. God said they tested and provoked Me.

Many of us still do that to God. We get up one day and sing God's praise, and the very next week when things don't look like we want them to, we start with "does Jesus care?" God is concerned about how our inconveniences prevent us from trusting Him. How many more things must God do for us before we determine that God is God? If we examine our agenda we are constantly complaining about what we don't have. If we could only learn to give thanks for all God has given us. One of God's big problems is trying to satisfy His people. Do you know anyone who cannot be satisfied? No matter what you do, it is never enough? God wondered why His people could not be thankful for the quail and manna, instead of acting like that never happened. God wanted His people to remember what they saw in Egypt— slavery, oppression and abuse. They wanted to go back to the garlic, onions and leeks— they thought that was good food. We are just like that. God saved us from the world and we know how the world messes over us. The world did have a few things we liked, things that turned us on. In spite of the fact that we needed to be delivered from it, we liked some feature of the things we needed to be delivered from. So, in difficult times we wonder if doing it the world's way would be beneficial. But God says there are onions and garlic but don't forget there is also slavery back in the world, too. That is why God took away some pleasures that He knew were destructive. Then verse 10 concluded the warning: "for forty years I loathed that generation" says God. The word loathe in Hebrew means to be disgusted with folks who just won't do right. God was disgusted for forty years with the same folks. Every day God took care of them, but they were never satisfied.

That is how God feels about some believers. He is disgusted because so much of what we do is religion retried. We do not go to God to worship Him; we go to sit on the pew to please ourselves. Why do you worship is the question. The answer should be because God wants to meet with me. Since God is patient with us, let us not destroy His tolerance. They were physically there in worship but their hearts were far from Him, neither did they do His works. The Bible says God's ways are not our ways, nor His thoughts our thoughts. Therefore, most of us should be sitting on the edge of our seats asking God to teach us His thoughts because we won't think that way unless He tells us. The reason we have to spend time in personal worship is to find out His way because the ways of the Lord are right. The conclusion of verse 11 suggests that the people will not enter into their rest because of God's anger. This is a depressing thought.

Why did God deliver Israel? To take them to the land of Canaan. What was in the land of Canaan? There was rest. Rest from what? Rest from their enemies, from the soul that would not produce. There was peace— God took the Israelites through the wilderness to get their focus on God. They had to learn how to trust God, despite the wilderness. So, if our lives are going in circles, there is a rest that belongs to the children of God. What is rest for us? Rest for us is the enjoyment of God in this life on a daily basis. God brings us to a spiritual point where we are able to relax in Him in spite of the situations in life. That is the promise that God gives, if we would let Him give it to us. In order to get this rest, we have to serve God in obedience. God gives rest when we worship God the way He wants to be worshipped. Worship is recognizing God for who He is, and when we recognize God to be God, then God will be God for us.

CHAPTER XII

THE FOCUS OF LOVE

From whence come wars and fightings among you? come they not hence, even of your lusts that war in your members?

Ye lust, and have not: ye kill, and desire to have, and cannot obtain: ye fight and war, yet ye have not, because ye ask not.

Ye ask, and receive not, because ye ask amiss, that ye may consume it upon your lusts.

Ye adulterers and adulteresses, know ye not that the friendship of the world is enmity with God? whosoever therefore will be a friend of the world is the enemy of God.

Do ye think that the scripture saith in vain, The spirit that dwelleth in us lusteth to envy?

But he giveth more grace. Wherefore he saith, God resisteth the proud, but giveth grace unto the humble.

Submit yourselves therefore to God. Resist the devil, and he will flee from you.

Draw nigh to God, and he will draw nigh to you. Cleanse your hands, ye sinners; and purify your hearts, ye double minded.
James 4:1-8

One tragic element in our Christian faith is two-timing Christians, who at one moment say that they love God with all their heart, soul and mind, and the next time you see them they have deserted their God. You can see how they are leaving God out of their lives, thoughts, and relationships. They neglect to seek

His guidance for direction. God can't tell them how to live and can't go with them where they go. It's as if they say, "God, stay here in the pew, and I will pick you up next week." Let's look at what God says to these Christians, in the book of James, chapter 4, who attempt to fake God out with Sunday morning appearances and attendance. He speaks to us who come to church and act as if everything is okay— those of us who pretend we have no problems. God knows we've been tipping around on Him come Monday. He sees how we change from being Dr. Jekyll to Mr. Hyde.

His message to them is that He is aware that He doesn't have their full attention during the week. But on Sunday these people become instant friends with God again. In all reality, God is speaking to those of us who are two-timing Him. He's speaking to Christians who say "Lord, I love you with all my heart. I'm thankful that you saved me. I want to live my life for you." However, by Monday they forget about Him.

Who is this character, this Mr. Hyde, the one whom God is so much against? It is called the world. But before going any further we must define the "world." Is the world simply being where sinners are? Are you in the world because you live, eat, and bank with sinners? Many of you live in neighborhoods which are harnessed on both sides by sinners. Is that what makes you worldly?

According to the Bible, the world is the system headed by Satan that leaves God out. To love the world means that you function in it without the presence of God. When you love the world God is left out as you go to work, dwell in your neighborhood, and even as you interact in your friendships. As you reflect on this, imagine God saying to you "In these relationships you are doing your own thing— going places where I can't go; saying things that I can't talk about; doing things that I can't participate in— then you come to church next Sunday testifying that you and I are doing all right." To this, God says that you profess your dedication on Sunday and yet leave Him sitting in the pew on Monday while you go do your thing. But God's response to you is that He can sit in the pew and still see where you go, and see what you do. He can sit right there and know that you have left Him out.

This is God's complaint. You have an intimacy with the world, which means that you are hostile towards Him. God says "I am no fool! I am not satisfied with just hearing the words I love you while you live your life, leaving Me out. No one else knows you are a Christian— except our friends in church." Many Christians need to realize that playing this role prevents us from standing up for Christian principles. We are poor representatives of Christ because we are too busy trying to compromise in order to be like the world. Before we know it, we have become Christian chameleons— changing colors according to what the world looks like.

God is saying that many of us are embarrassed to have Him as our main friend, even embarrassed to identify with Him. God says "I am angry that you are trying to do a number on Me. You told me that you would cherish Me and function only through Me. You said that I would be the only love of your life, yet you go out and chase after other loves, and then ask me, "what's wrong?" From Monday to Saturday you do your own thing and then expect Me to flip because you showed up in church Sunday morning. I'm supposed to get ecstatic, happy, say look who's here? No dice! This is not love, it's hostility and I am angry about that!"

God reacts to desertion. God reacts to one-day commitment. God reacts to attitudes that say one thing and demonstrate something else. God uses this dualism of human desire to talk about the focus of our love. The focus of love as God talks about it is based on the fact that you can only love Him. "Thou shalt have no other gods before Me." Yet, what we have are Christians who sit on this invisible fence, with one leg in the world and the other in church, and what they do is politely shift at the right time, rocking back and forth, from side to side because they want to have the best of both worlds.

How do you know if you have fallen out of love? The writer James says one way to tell is if there is a lot of confusion in your life. Whenever we have conflict, it is usually because of our own desires and our willingness to compromise our values. Such Christians want the good times, living for the gusto— but they don't know that in order to live like the world, they have to become like the world. When you look at relationships, most conflicts arise because both persons want to win. The attitude is that I must be the winner and I must outperform everyone because the goal of my life is "me." There are so many relational problems that could be solved if both parties agree that they don't have to win. As long as there are groups where everyone has to win, accomplishing their own pleasures and goals, there will be conflict. The corporate ladder is climbed in conflict because of the dog-eat-dog view of the world. We justify this by proclaiming "that's the way of the world!" However, that attitude of having to be the winner will always create head-on conflict in our relationship with God because we can't top God in anything, especially in knowing what's best for us. God says "Don't bring that junk into My kingdom. In My kingdom there is only one love. Therefore, if I'm the only love in that kingdom there should be no conflict because everything is being done for one reason— to glorify Me and to advance My kingdom.

Another reason there is conflict is that we have chosen another way to do our thing. We lust, meaning we want it bad. Some of us want some things so badly and we can't wait that we break our necks to get it. God says we lust and are still not satisfied with the things or relationships we end up with. We do everything possible to get that thing or person, and what we get is not what we bargained for. We lust and do not have so we commit murder! James is not saying that Christians were carrying guns or knives to church. However, Jesus says, "thou shall not commit murder, but anyone who hates his brother commits murder already." Therefore, James is talking about the attitude which leads to the act. The attitude presupposes the action, and James is saying when we try to do things the worldly way, we compromise and become like them in order to satisfy our needs.

Many people say that it is a rough world out there. That stuff in the Bible can't be used on Monday, it is too soft for such a hard world! However, the Bible clearly states that "you have not because you ask not." God says you break your neck trying to love the world when all you have to do is ask your main lover. If you just spend some time with God and ask Him, He will gladly give it away. What God is saying is that we are trying to get the world to fix up our lives when all we really need to do is spend some time with Him; then all we have to do is ask. It takes the pressure off— it takes the frustration away— it eliminates the anxiety because He is the provider of all our needs. God says invest your time with Me and all you have to do is ask. God wants us to have such a love affair where we just ask. But if we don't, we will have to fight for it. Personally, I had to fight and scratch my way to the top. I won over them before they won over me. That's the way you get to the top.

James suggests that some of us pray and never receive for the sole reason that we ask with the wrong motives. Our intent is to spend it on pleasure. If God gives us what we ask for, we will love the gift more than the giver; then there will be something else for us to put in His place as we push Him out. The scenario goes something like this: "Lord, give me that house— so that you cannot come in." "Lord, give me that car— so that you can't ride in it." "Lord, give me that money— so you can't use it. Give it to me so I can use it for me." To such statements I can imagine God saying, "You've got to be kidding. I will not give you anything which will let you leave Me out and use it solely for your pleasure." God is no fool. Therefore, He will tell us no at times in order to remind us that when we accepted Him as Lord, we told Him we would be His alone. Yet, some of us will still try to argue with, "but I was in church last Sunday." To which God replies, "I didn't marry you for Sunday, but I married you for a relationship and an intimacy that should be experienced every day.

You can leave God out and do well: be a millionaire or have a good business, but there will come a time when God will not make Himself available. When you come back, the locks will be changed and you'll have to spend some time in the cold. This is why God gets so many casualties. They are those who come back after being beaten up by the world.

We need to know that God loves us and wants a relationship. God is jealous about the spirit He has put in us. Like any good love relationship— He does not want to share us with the world. Consequently, we need to realize that Satan is bothered when we carry throughout the entire week the ideas and principles which we learned in church. We actually infiltrate his territory with the love we have. God says "I'm jealous and I want to go with you wherever you go. Can I go with you? Can I take part in your conversations? Can I look at what you are admiring? I'm jealous, and you can't leave Me out of your life and expect our relationship to thrive."

What difference will it make having God as our only focus? In verse 6, He gives a greater grace, "He opposes the proud but gives grace to the humble." We will have a love affair with God that will give us more grace. Grace is God doing for us what we cannot do for ourselves. As we keep living we will all run into situations where we will need God to do for us what we cannot do for ourselves. Right now, you can pay cash if you need to. Right now, everything seems to be going well. Right now, your health is fine, but there will come a time when only the grace of God can deliver you out of a situation, and unless there is a tight relationship, that extra grace will be missing! We will need God to be there, and God will send us to where we have always gotten our pleasure. Remember that He resists the proud— it is that attitude of pride that God works against. God says "I will decide not to participate in your life, and let's see what will happen. I am going to oppose." There will come a time when each of us will need some grace, and the outcome will be determined by how faithful we have been in our love affair with God.

So what should be done? James 4:6 says submit and resist. Submission to God means that you place yourself under divine authority, saying Lord whatever you want me to do I will do. What you will begin saying is no to Satan, bearing in mind that he will not leave you easily. The more submitted we are to God, the more the devil will attempt to interfere in the relationship to try to break it up or tear it down— but there comes a point when even the devil will run away. Many people say "I'm trying to get the devil off my back but he won't leave me alone." If the devil is bothering you that much, there is a spiritual problem. For Jesus says that if you are submitted to Him and the devil is riding your back, there comes a point where He will knock him off. If the devil is beating you up all the time, then you need to check your submission.

How do we submit? Verse 8 says draw near to God and He will draw near to you. That is the relationship. God would like to respond to us, but we have to draw near to Him.

How do we draw near? Verse 9 says cleanse our hands; get our lives together. We cannot draw near while we are doing our own thing. Wash your hands and move on with God alone.

God says it is no laughing matter if I am not your main focus. In fact, you should start crying now or you will surely be crying later. Therefore, it is time to humble yourself. Try something new— believe the Word of God. Try bowing all the way down to the authority of God and make sure your love is focused. Try saying with sincerity, "I want to love You alone, God, so that Your grace can be available to me."

You may ask what is the focus of love? It is Jesus Christ alone. There is no room for anyone else, and the moment someone else enters we lose focus. There will come a time when we will need His grace. It will not be wise to let our rooms be empty at that time.

CHAPTER XIII

EXALTING GOD

**Having therefore, brethren, boldness to enter into
the holiest by the blood of Jesus,**

**By a new and living way, which he hath consecrated
for us, through the veil, that is to say, his flesh;**

And having an high priest over the house of God;

**Let us draw near with a true heart in full assurance
of faith, having our hearts sprinkled from an evil
conscience, and our bodies washed with pure water.**

**Let us hold fast the profession of our faith without
wavering; (for he is faithful that promised;)**

**And let us consider one another to provoke unto
love and to good works:**

**Not forsaking the assembling of ourselves together,
as the manner of some is; but exhorting one
another: and so much the more, as ye see the day
approaching.**

Hebrews 10:19-25

The author of Hebrews is writing primarily to Jewish
Christians who are torn between their newly developed allegiance
to Christ and their old commitment to the old covenant of the
Mosaic law.   They were card-carrying Old Testament Jews
committed to the Old Testament system. Jesus Christ appears on
the scene as the fulfillment of the Old Testament system, and He
informs them that faith in Him is the way they have a relationship
with God. It is no longer by offering lambs and heifers but it is
through the profession of faith in Christ. Many of the Jews started
to latch on to Jesus but the old neighborhood was still around.
They still had the old crowd pulling them back to Judaism, pulling

them back to the Tabernacle and Old Testament sacrifices and old laws. So, on one hand they had the new commitment to Christ, but on the other hand they had the old crowd pulling them back. The Book of Hebrews was written to tell the Jews don't turn back because when you met Jesus you took a major leap forward. Why if you were promoted to the president of the company would you go back to being the janitor? The Old Testament laws and rituals have fulfilled their purpose. Throughout this book Paul gives a lot of time outs where God calls the Jewish believers to respond to the warning of not turning back.

Paul admonishes the Jews to take a time out from a system which Jesus is getting ready to destroy. Do you know why the Bible instructs Christians to turn away from the world when they come to Christ? In I John 2, John puts it this way: "for all that is in the world is the lust of the flesh, the lust of the eye, and the pride of life," and this world is passing away. It is under divine sentence, so don't go back.

There is one thing worse then being a sinner, and that is being a Christian living like a sinner, because now we have God in our lives. As a result of living a dual life, there are two miserable people: you and God. God will let us know that He is not happy with the way things are going. Do you notice when there is confusion on the football field the quarterback says "time out— let's get this straight. The play is messed up?" The writer of Hebrews says "time out because you are going in the wrong direction." So many people are going in the wrong direction being caught in the tension of wanting to go with God but the world is pulling— not lightly either— and dragging their arm out of the armpits. The world has no mercy on its desire to have us. The writer tells them that a proper focus on God— worship— and then a proper relationship to God's people— caring— is the mechanism by which people keep on keeping on. We just can't make it on our own as Christians. Many of us have found out that although we are saved, things do not come up roses. In all reality, Satan, who was our best friend before we became Christians, has now become our worst enemy, and he wants us to know it. Therefore, in the book of James we have this warning: "don't feel surprised when trials come upon you." That's just the way it's going to be, for we cannot live in the midst of hell looking like heaven and not expect the fire to scorch us. Yet, Paul says your focus will be the key to pull you through the trials. He put it in a context of worship, starting with verse 19 of Chapter 10. In talking about the sufficiency of Christ, the author did not explain much, for he assumes that the readers already knew because they were Jewish people completely saturated and consumed by the Old Testament. He says we can have confidence when we enter the holy place through Jesus Christ. When a Jewish person heard this, however, what did they think? He thought you must be crazy! Why? Because nobody has confidence to enter the holy place but the High Priest— and that's only once a year!

Back in the Old Testament there was a temple or tabernacle that had a court area which led to the Holy of Holies. In front of the Holy of Holies was the veil; behind the Holy of Holies was the Ark of the Covenant, and that is where God's glory rested. People did not go beyond the veil. They did not have direct access to being in the presence of the living God. Once a year one man was given the privilege to go beyond that veil. The priest would atone for the sins of the people beyond the veil, and they would consider it going into the presence of God. Now, here comes the author of Hebrews telling these people the good news that you can now go directly into the presence of the living God because of the blood of Jesus.

What the blood of Jesus does is gives us the right to walk unashamed into the presence of God, knowing that nothing will happen to us. In the Old Testament you would die. However, in the New Testament if we come by the blood of Christ, it is as if God says, "Come on in. What took you so long?" He explains it by a new and living way. New in the sense that the Old Testament did not have this provision because it is based on the life of Jesus Christ and what Christ inaugurated, which is His blood shed at Calvary. When they crucified Him, there was no beauty in Him. When you read the account, He was brutally beaten and a crown of thorns was placed on His head as His blood came out like gushing water. When we understand that the tearing of His body was God's way of saying "come on in," how can one stay home? How can we not enter into the presence of God individually when we understand that they veil of the temple was torn by the veil of His flesh being torn? Now we understand why Paul says time out because it cost our Lord too much to let the world win the deal. Paul wants us to know we no longer need a human priest to bring our confession to God. There is no longer a need for an authoritarian to represent our need before God. We already have such a person, and He sits right next to the One we are trying to get to. With this High Priest, we do not have to worry if He is in fellowship with God or off in a foreign land.

The following story is told by a lady who went to confession. It was time for the priest to go to lunch as the lady approached the confession booth. She begged him to hear her cry, but the priest said, "Sorry. I will be back at 1 p.m." However, with our High Priest we don't have to worry about a lunch hour or dinner time. Jesus says "Come on in. I've opened the door for you." If you are losing to the pull of this world it is because you have not walked in the very presence of God.

Then the author comes to the core of what he wants us to know in verse 22. He challenges us to "draw near to God." Let me say that God is never far away, though we may be far away from Him. Paul's exhortation is for us to come closer to God. God says if we are losing to the world it is because we are not drawing near to Him. That is also why parents would tell their children to be careful of who you run with, realizing that who they spend time with will influence their lives. God says it depends on what you draw near to. Here, the author is telling the Jews if you are still spending time with the Old Testament system, but show up on Sunday to come to the church of the New Testament believer, sure you will lose out. What we need to do then is draw near to Him only.

So, it's a matter of focus on which way we are drawing and the way we talk that will determine where we spend our time and energy. If our time and energy is with the world, i.e. our perspective is that which leaves God out, our orientation to life will leave God out. That is what I mean by the world, not the physical environment.

There are some criteria about how to draw near to God. Some people say, "I've tried to draw near to God, and He is not there." If that is the case, then we need to draw near in the right way. We should draw near with a sincere heart. We cannot want to play the religious games with God and fool around on Him, wanting Him to accept the fact that we have another friend consuming our attention. We have to be genuine in our desire to go with God all the way. If we draw near without that commitment, we have not drawn near at all.

The question here is how exactly do we draw near? It should be with sincerity from within the inner person. We must come to God, taking Him seriously. God is not a big buddy or Santa Claus in the sky. God is God and He demands to be taken seriously by His people because of what it cost Him to provide for our salvation. He continues in verse 22 to deal with both the inner and outer cleaning. He challenges us to be for real internally, totally committed to Him, and not just presenting an external presence. We have to deal with the sin in our lives. That is what Holy Communion was designed to do. Then we should have our bodies washed with pure water. Here he is talking about living out the cleanliness that we articulated in our baptism: outward clean living based on inward clean living. What we want to do is one of two things. We want to live terrible on the outside but still say our hearts are right, using the expression "the Lord knows my heart." The reality is the Lord knows our heart but sees our body. What God says is that what is in our hearts should be expressed by what is in our bodies. The Bible says our bodies are the temples of the Living God. So, we cannot have a right heart and the wrong body. It is erroneous to suggest that God understands our hearts because God's concern is what is in our heart does not get transferred to our feet. It is imperative that we transfer our Sunday worship experience to Monday because people do not see our hearts, they see our bodies. The thing that is to mark the household of faith is that they are engaged in a different kind of walk. Some of us have been in church for a long time but have not made much progress on the outside but claim that God is doing it on the inside. God's whole point is to get it on the outside so His message can impact the world.

Verse 23 suggests that we should hold fast the confession of God because He who promises is faithful. The author says the reason we can endure is because God doesn't lie: He says what He means and means what He says. God has not lied to us. This leads us into the caring mode. If God provides the power and tells us to endure without going back to the pain and emptiness of the past, the question becomes how is this possible? Verse 24 answers this: "Let us stimulate one another to love and good deeds." Let's take the first one. That word stimulate is a strong word. To stimulate means to provoke. Do you have anybody in your life who provokes you? Every time they say something they seem to initiate a fight. The word stimulate has the idea of provoking, getting on your nerves. It is a word used negatively in the New Testament, using one's words or actions negatively for destructive reasons. But here we have the admonition to provoke one another for good deeds. God understands that He is invisible. Though we can't see God, He is giving these visible instructions from His invisible temple.

The question is how do I get this invisible God to energize us, remind us, provoke us, and stimulate us to endure to the end? What we discover is that God's provokers are other Christians. The church is designed to develop relationships of people who get on your nerves for the Kingdom. Believers should develop strategies to get us on a move to be about good works. It is the job of God's people to provoke one another to hold on. Whenever a believer is getting ready to fall, fellow Christians should always admonish them to hold on. It is when we are out there and nobody is telling us to hold on that causes us to say, "Then why hold on?" When we became a part of the church, we joined a network of strategies to get those who are straying.

As believers, we are responsible to each other. The word love means to seek the highest good of another even though it may be an inconvenience. To stimulate one another not only aids the helpee but also the helper. It allows us to take the focus off ourselves and put it on someone else.

How shall we stimulate one another into good deeds? Verse 25 says "don't forsake the assembly of yourselves together." Why? Because there is potency we can get in the group that we cannot get by ourselves. It is the community that provokes a response in all of us. What God is saying is the community provides the context of moving on. So when we separate from the community of God's people we are setting ourselves up to take on Satan by ourselves. We cannot do that. It is the community that provokes response. One of the problems with American Christianity is there are no communities. We get into our individual cars, drive down our individual streets to get to our individual churches to sit in my individual pew. We listen to individual sermons and return to my individual home. That is not New Testament Christianity. Christianity is where God's children are called into a community just like a family. God did not save us for ourselves but for each one to stimulate the person who is near to us. The idea of going to church is to see what God has for us so we can stimulate each other, and in turn, the church can achieve its goal. When we leave a caring environment, the church should be there. Then, when what we have invited on ourselves is the loss of any dynamic presence of God in our lives, and when we need Him, God will be available to us.

Then the author closes with some powerful ideas. He reminds us that the Church is not a perfect institution. The church is where we assemble because everything is wrong and we need a family who understands. We can come in not having to lie about what we are feeling and thinking and they won't walk away from me. People like to feel at home and the good news is, if you are a Christian, you are at home. Don't forsake the assembly of yourselves because when the world is destroyed, it will not turn around to help us. That is why the last line says "especially as we see the last day approaching."

In the Bible there is what is called the near view and the far view of prophesy, i.e., a prophetic utterance given that has both an immediate and a long-distance application. That is what we have here. The author is writing to the Jews. Jesus had prophesied before His death that the temple would be destroyed. The Book of Hebrews was written just a few years before the Roman General Titus descended on Jerusalem and wiped out the remnant of Jewish worship in 70 A.D. The day of God's judgment was approaching and he says, "Christians get away from the temple. The temple will be destroyed. Christians, why hold on to the world? God is going to destroy it as we approach the second coming of our Lord," which is the far view. There are constant, destructive problems that never get solved. What we are witnessing is the stage being set for the return of Jesus Christ. How are Christians going to make it? We are God's people who belong to a community that supports each other. We need to develop methodology to sustain each other because we need each other.

CHAPTER XIV

WHAT ARE YOU BRAGGING ABOUT?

For a voice of wailing is heard out of Zion, How are we spoiled! we are greatly confounded, because we have forsaken the land, because our dwellings have cast us out.

Yet hear the word of the LORD, O ye women, and let your ear receive the word of his mouth, and teach your daughters wailing, and every one her neighbour lamentation.

For death is come up into our windows, and is entered into our palaces, to cut off the children from without, and the young men from the streets.

Speak, Thus saith the LORD, Even the carcases of men shall fall as dung upon the open field, and as the handful after the harvestman, and none shall gather them.

Thus saith the LORD, Let not the wise man glory in his wisdom, neither let the mighty man glory in his might, let not the rich man glory in his riches:

But let him that glorieth glory in this, that he understandeth and knoweth me, that I am the LORD which exercise lovingkindness, judgment, and righteousness, in the earth: for in these things I delight, saith the LORD.

Behold, the days come, saith the LORD, that I will punish all them which are circumcised with the uncircumcised;

Jeremiah 9:23-26

Most of us commit the sin of placing things in our lives ahead of God. They become more important than our personal relationship with Him. When this happens, we will meditate on everything but God. Many of us know so much about various aspects of life but very little about God. The reason we become so knowledgeable in any particular area is because we study. Whatever a person studies is what he/she comes to know and thus it occupies his/her mind.

God says nothing, not even the good things in life, are ever to replace knowing Him. The answer is the same to all of the following questions:

Why were we created? To know God.
What will we be doing forever? Knowing God.
What is the thing that makes life valuable?

Knowledge of God.

What is the ultimate goal of existence? Knowing God.

That is why Jeremiah writes to the generation of his day: "Thus says the Lord let not the wise boast in his wisdom; rich in his riches; mighty in his might." Boast in the fact of your knowledge of God.

Now, I have a question for you: Do you know God? I am not asking whether you know about God or whether your parents know about Him. I am not asking whether you can recite a verse from His word, nor am I asking if you know doctrines. When we speak of knowing someone we are defining what makes another person tick, and how that affects us. When a person knows his/her spouse, they are able to do things in the other's absence with the confidence that had their partner been there, he/she would do the same thing. To know someone does not mean that you have met them, for I have known many people whom I have not met.

There are three possible groups of people in which most of you readers can be classified. As you continue reading, determine whether you are among:

(a) Those who do not know God and have not met Him and are totally isolated from God. Though they have heard about Him, and know He exists, He is a stranger to them. Many people fit into this category and because they know He exists, they think they know Him. For example, you may think you know President Clinton because of the newspapers, or television. However, that is not knowledge of the President; that is merely information. Many people know God to the same extent: they know He is there but have never met Him.

(b) Those who have met Him but do not yet know Him. In other words, one day they heard the Gospel and accepted the Good News. Christ came into their lives to be their Savior. At that moment they met God. A meeting took place.

(c) Those who met God and have just begun to know Him. When God met them and they became Christians, the purpose of the meeting was to prompt them to know Him. God did not reach them so that they might meet Him. For some, meeting God has become an end in itself. Therefore, if we fall in this group we cannot talk about what God is doing in our lives right now. The only thing we ever talk about is what happened when we met Him. Just like a couple who only talks about what happened when they first met. They got married and have experienced no growth or real joy since then. All the good times occurred at the beginning of the relationship. It is apparent that many Christians are in this group.

Whenever you acknowledge someone's expertise, it is because they appear to know their subject(s) better than anyone else. If the expert knows his subject well, you can become the listener, he becomes the teacher and learning takes place. However, if you do too much talking in front of the expert, you will be embarrassed for saying what you do not know. The higher a person is in their knowledge of what they are about, the more compelling it is to listen to them. It is annoying to see how little listening time God gets from us, although we agree He is the expert.

Does anyone know God better than God? No. How much of God is there to know? Too much for any mortal human to comprehend. Do you know what we will be doing forever in Heaven? Knowing God. The thing that will get heaven excited will be our knowing God. The primary topic of conversation will be knowing God. What do I mean when I say knowing God? This is our problem and the complaint of God! We don't understand what it means to know God. If we did, then we would understand that heaven could never be boring. The reason we do not get excited about knowing God is that on earth the individual process of knowing God is constantly interrupted. In heaven, there will be no interruptions, and Jesus will shine like the sun, and every day will be an opportunity to see what God will come up with next. But, God does not want us to have to wait until we get to heaven to be exposed to or to get an idea of the splendor of knowing Him. He wants us to get some practice right now. Jeremiah said: If you are going to brag about anything in life— it is better that you know God.

One day a friend went to a farmer's house, and he noticed the farmer had been using the door of his barn as a target range and every bullet was in the bull's-eye. He saw the man had shot all ten bull's-eyes ten times, right in the middle of each eye! In amazement, the friend said "Wow, you sure can shoot! You are tremendous! Have you thought about entering competition? You shoot so straight." The farmer responded, "Friend, you don't understand. I shoot the bullet first and then I mark the bull's-eye." That is the way most people live— they shoot and then they circle the bull's-eye and say that is what life is all about. If you are like most people, the habit is to develop your own meaning of life, and whatever you are going after becomes the bull's-eye. God attacks this and says "let not the rich, whose bull's-eye is riches— or the powerful boast in power— or the wise whose bull's-eye is intellectual degrees brag about these things because all are targets created by humans. What God wants to know is not whether we can hit our bull's-eyes, but can we hit His. God's bull's-eye is the knowledge of God. If we are not hitting that, we are missing life.

Most people do not know who they are because God has made it so that there can be no definition of who we are without knowing who God is. Answer this: who are you? I am not asking who are you in terms of a description such as 5'9", 180 lbs.— because that is describing yourself and I want you to define yourself. In order to do that, you cannot say I am black, or describe what you have, who your parents are, where you live, etc. Therefore, what you will discover is that most people do not know who they are. God has made us in the image of who He is, and that is why nothing we have will ever tell us who we are.

In verse 23, Jeremiah says do not boast in your wisdom. Do not boast in that fact that you have accumulated certain intellectual skills that allow you to manage in life. The reason you should not brag is that no matter how much intellect you have, you will run into some type of roadblock in life and the only thing that can bail you out will be what you know about God. There are things which you will face in life that cannot be resolved in the library or in study books. Things will go wrong that medical science cannot answer. The best minds are looking at the world and saying there is no hope. Jeremiah is saying you are educated, graduated with Bachelors or Masters degree— congratulations!— but do not brag about it.

Do not boast because you have might: you have a new job, now you are a supervisor, and all of a sudden the personality shifts. It is no longer ours— it's yours, you have clout now. You have control of things and you call the shots. You are on top now. God does not condemn us for being on top, but God serves notice: Do not brag. Don't get pumped up!

Jeremiah was speaking to a bragging Israel who thought they had become a mighty nation. However, there comes a time when God will humble you, and it does not matter how powerful you are. Isaiah says: God looked over the nation and they looked as grasshoppers, and He merely looked on them causing them to whither. Compared to God, our power is nothing. The problem for people with power today is that they lack perspective. That is why the Bible says employers should deal justly with their employees— because the employer has a greater employer in heaven. God clearly lets you know that you are not to brag if you have power.

The third point made in this verse is that you should not brag because you have money— or as he says, "let not the rich man boast in his riches." Like many of us, you like to show off when you have on new clothes. But, God says that you are not to go around puffed up just because you may have more than your fellow man. God says if you brag, brag that you know Him or you will soon forget how you were able to get what you have.

If we do not have knowledge of God, then the very blessing we receive may be that which destroys us later on. We can all probably think of people to whom this has happened. I have gone to small one-bedroom homes which are filled with joy. And I have gone to large houses where there is constant conflict. There will come a time when something will hit your life and not even money will be able to buy you out of it. For example, when your doctor announces that the disease is incurable— you can't take out your checkbook. We need to know God, not a checkbook. When your teenage child tells you that he/she is leaving and no longer needs you, what you'll need more than anything is to know God.

The question in this chapter is do you know God? God says let him who boasts do two things: 1) understand and 2) know Me. To understand is to make sense of your knowledge of Me so that when you read My Word you will use it to make a difference in your human situations, your every day life, because you now have new information about Me. What can you say that you know? He is Lord and He is personal, not just some force that exists. God has feelings and carries out action. If you know His feelings and action, you will know that He is a personal God to you.

First, Jeremiah names three things that God does: He is the Lord, exercising lovingkindness. God is the epitome of love. He told Israel, I have a commitment to you, even if you are not committed to Me. Judgment will fall but I still love you. Israel had been immoral, but God says I will still love you. If God acted in unfaithfulness towards us like we act towards Him, then we would never thank Him. He is loyal love. God is not unfaithful toward us like we are toward Him. His love is the kind that will discipline you sternly, but at the same time says come home.

Second, the Lord is also a God of justice. God assures us that what goes around comes around, and when He deals with the world He will deal justly. There are certain injustices carried out in this world which will not be corrected in our lifetime. But justice must begin with Christians now. For some reason we believe that God should start with sinners first. What we forget is that man will be spending eternity separated from God, but God wants to get us ready for heaven now. We do not discipline people's children as we do our own because they don't live in our house. Justice starts in God's house.

Finally, He is also a God of righteousness. The only way we can determine righteousness is by knowing God because He is— by definition— righteous. Knowing God tells us what is right, and most of us do not know what is right because we do not know God. God is frustrated when His children do not want to get to know Him.

What does all this mean? Where do you go from here? You must make a decision on whether you want to know God. Here are some steps to try to achieve:

(a)   Make time to listen to Him talk to you. You should not have devotion just to have it, but have it because you want to know God, taking time to meditate on His Word.

(b)   Make an appointment with God and keep it.

As Daniel Whittle and the great traditional hymn suggests,

> I do not know why God's wondrous grace to me hath made known, nor why unworthy Christ in love redeemed me for His own
>
> I know not what of good or ill may be reserved for me of weary ways or golden days before I see His face.
>
> But I know whom I believed and am persuaded that
>
> He is able to keep that which I've committed unto Him against that day.